DEI DOLPHINS?

THE STORY OF "PROJECT SHORT TIME"

To Mikey Regs,

A Brief History of the U.S. Navy's

First Marine Mammal Swimmer Defense System

Hope you enjoy Learning about our NAVY Dolphins!

U.S NAVY CAPT (RET)

HAROLD W. GOFORTH, JR., PH.D.

with Anita K. Palmer

Hal W. Goforth Jr   *3/20/2018*

HG.

FORTIS

A NON-FICTION IMPRINT FROM ADDUCENT

Adducent, Inc.

www.Adducent.Co

Titles Distributed In

North America

United Kingdom

Western Europe

South America

Australia

PRAISE FOR *DEFENDER DOLPHINS*

Over time, U.S. secrets come to light — through loose lips or declassification. The latter has resulted in Hal Goforth's detailed and fascinating account of a clandestine effort undertaken decades ago during the Vietnam war, to protect military assets from underwater threats. A security system relying on the most intelligent of marine creatures — the dolphin — proved successful in accomplishing this mission, a story now told by one personally involved.

> — *LCOL James G. Zumwalt, USMC (Ret), Author of Bare Feet, Iron Will—Stories from the Other Side of Vietnam's Battlefields*

In recent years, the public has come to appreciate the remarkable ability of service dogs to protect our military in the deserts, cities and mountains. There is another animal group that has long gone unnoticed and underappreciated – the U.S. Navy dolphins that have protected our military at sea for the past fifty years. Hal Goforth's remarkable story details for the first time the partnership forged between man and dolphins in service during the Vietnam war. Melding history, dolphin biology, and behavior, and an insider's view of a military mission, Dr. Goforth takes the reader on a unique journey where military lives depend on the intelligence and steadfastness of one of the ocean's most personable animals and the U.S. Navy's biggest secret.

> — *Terrie M. Williams., PhD, Professor of Ecology and Evolutionary Biology, University of California, Santa Cruz, author of* The Odyssey of Kp2: An Orphan Seal, A Marine Biologist, and the Fight to Save a Species *(Penguin Press, 2012).*

I am the creator and co-author of the Flipper story. I trained "Mitzi," the first dolphin to swim with a human in the open ocean. Mitzi was used in the first *Flipper* movie. I also trained "Susie," who was in the second movie, *Flipper's New Adventure* and the first dolphin used in the TV series *Flipper*.

Having worked with dolphins for years, I believe we have only scratched the surface understanding their level of intelligence. I believe *Defender Dolphins* would be of great interest to readers regarding the use of dolphins by the U.S. Navy and their exploits in the Vietnam conflict.

— *Ricou Browning, Dolphin Trainer, Creator and Co-Author of Flipper*

Defender Dolphins reveals how a handful of dedicated scientists, engineers and biologists came together to confront one of the most difficult challenges the Navy faced in Vietnam, and still faces today. Hal Goforth tells the truth about how the Navy effectively used dolphins to protect its fleet at Cam Ranh Bay, Vietnam, during the heat of the Vietnam War. His knowledge of the Navy's first Swimmer Defense System is unsurpassed.

— *Ron Seiple, CAPT (Ret), a decorated two-time Vietnam Veteran Navy SEAL, and former Science Advisor for the Commander Pacific Fleet who was considered one of the Navy's experts in Swimmer Defense Systems.*

DEFENDER DOLPHINS

The Story of "Project Short Time"
By U.S Navy CAPT (Ret) Harold W. Goforth, Jr., Ph.D.
with Anita K. Palmer

ISBN: 978-19375923-0-1

Cover Photo by Terry Rioux

Back Cover Artwork by Jim Cory

A Fortis book published by Adducent

Adducent, Inc.
Jacksonville, Florida
www.Adducent.Co

This is a work of non-fiction. No names have been changed, no characters invented, no events fabricated. During the 10 years I worked on this book, I conducted countless hours interviewing managers, scientists, engineers, trainers, veterinarians, and Navy personnel who lived the events of this story. They have made this story possible. In addition, I relied on published books, articles, military reports, dissertations, theses, and reliable websites. I also referred to entries in a personal logbook I kept during this story and that of Milo McManus. Whenever possible, I conducted recorded interviews and made countless phone calls or sent emails to confirm details. I was generously given access to many official Navy photographs and reports that augmented my photos and those of other participants in this story. In attempting to re-create events that occurred more than forty years ago, I was frequently re-minded how long ago all this happened and that many memories have faded completely or become unclear at best. I apologize in advance for omissions and/or errors in facts. I have done my best with the assistance of many, but in the end I am responsible for this story. I hope the reader becomes informed and enlightened, and at times may smile at these true events. These marine mammals have amazing capabilities. We have much more to learn from them.

— *Harold W. Goforth, Jr., Ph.D.*

DEDICATION

This book is dedicated to the managers, scientists, engineers, veterinarians, trainers, and military personnel of Project Short Time, and to the defender dolphins, especially Toad.

The author with Toad. San Diego, 2006. *(U.S. Navy. Used by permission.)*

CONTENTS

II. THE ADVANCE MARINE BIOLOGICAL
SYSTEMS BEGIN (1968-1969) 35

DEFENDER DOLPHINS

The Story of "Project Short Time"

By U.S Navy CAPT (Ret) Harold W. Goforth, Jr., Ph.D.

with Anita K. Palmer

PREFACE

JUST AFTER MIDNIGHT ON 23 JUNE 1969, A YOUNG US Navy Ltjg. EOD diver quietly slipped over the side of a sixteen-foot Boston Whaler into the tropical waters off Key West. He knew bull sharks were common in these warm waters so he was a bit nervous and especially alert.

He had made a number of nighttime swims before, but this was his first in this channel. A gentle current assisted him as he swam in the main channel off the western end of the island. Here the waters of Florida Bay and the Atlantic Ocean meet, and at times the tidal currents can be strong.

He wore only his tan Navy-issued UDT swim trunks and "duck feet" fins. There was no need for SCUBA gear, a wet suit, a mask or a snorkel. He wasn't even wearing his K-bar knife tonight. The only metal on him was the D-ring buckle of his swim trunks.

Several times during the swim he was startled when brushed by clumps of drifting turtle grass or a large tarpon rolling a few feet away. Nevertheless, he swam silently, never lifting his hands above the water and being careful not to make a splash. He was simulating a Vietnamese swimmer sapper.

At some point, without warning, his swim ended abruptly when he was soundly thumped in the back by a dolphin.

I was that swimmer. I did not know it then, but I would become the Navy's first Marine Mammal Officer. The dolphin was an Atlantic bottlenose dolphin (*Tursiops truncatus*), one of five dolphins captured in the Florida Keys and initially trained by civilians at the Naval Undersea Center's Hawaii Laboratory and later by Navy personnel. The dolphins' names were Garth, John, Slan, Tinker and Toad. You'll meet them in this book.

This would be the first of countless times over the next two years that I would make this swim. The location, waters, and targets would vary slightly but the swims would all start and end the same way. I would be dropped off from a small boat, and then hold on to a channel buoy or tread water for a while. Next I would swim several hundred yards towards a target, usually a ship or pier — as a Vietnamese swimmer sapper would, in an attempt to attack a US Navy asset during the Vietnam War.

Sapper swimmer attacks were Rear Admiral Elmo R. (Bud) Zumwalt's biggest problem in Vietnam. A year and half later, I and three other EOD officers, plus 18 highly trained and dedicated (mostly EOD) sailors, would provide a solution, using the Navy's history-making first operational Marine Mammal System deployed to a war zone.

A Story that Needed Telling

This book is a non-fiction, historical account covering the years 1960-1972, documenting how this system was developed and deployed to Vietnam. In these pages, I also review early marine mammal research at the Naval Missile Center (NMC) Point Mugu Bioscience Facility. It was there that marine mammal capabilities were studied, and the first sea lion and dolphins trained for open-ocean release. It was here that swimmer detection "proof-of-concept" tests using dolphins were conducted. I also examine the efforts by determined civilian scientists to radically expand their basic marine mammal research to include US Navy applications (for example, swimmer defense, object recovery and later mine location and neutralization systems).

This book also details the history of Project STROMAC and Project Short Time (both classified SECRET until 1992). It documents the design, development, technical and operational evaluations of Project Short Time conducted at the Naval Undersea Center's Hawaii Laboratory, Key West, and Vietnam. It includes an account of the twelve-month deployment and successful swimmer defense of a strategic ammunition pier at Cam Ranh Bay, Vietnam as Coastal Task Unit 115.9.1.

Destined to Write the Account

Why did I write this book? The simple answer is that this story had to be told, and I believe that I was destined to write it. There were just too many coincidences that occurred in my life that allowed me to be involved with Project Short Time and to have known and worked closely with many of the primary players in this very amazing story.

This account of Project Short Time (also referred to as the Dolphin Swimmer Defense System) has been written in good faith with every attempt to verify facts and honestly represent actual conversations. The information comes from two main sources. First, I spent hundreds of hours interviewing the Navy civilians; the principle project manager, marine mammal veterinarians, marine mammal scientists, trainers and engineers who conducted the research and designed and built the supporting equipment for the Navy's Marine Mammal Program. I also interviewed military and support personnel who deployed this system. Second, I turned to my personal logbooks, photographs, notes and memories I have as the first Navy officer assigned to Project STROMAC (later Short Time) and two years as a Marine Mammal Officer. This included four months in Cam Ranh Bay, Vietnam, as Assistant O-in-C of Project Short Time.

Writing a book like this before 1992 was impossible because until then this marine mammal system was classified SECRET. To this day, only two books have been written by persons who played important roles in the early history of this research and had firsthand knowledge of this Dolphin Swimmer Defense System.[1, 2]

A Foundation for Future Research

During my twenty-six-year Navy career (active and reserve duty), I was involved with the Navy's marine mammal programs to varying degrees. I monitored several long distance air transports of marine mammals and Operational Readiness Inspections of the MK-6 system (Project Short time). My Ph.D. dissertation at UCLA in 1985 documented the energy metabolism and force production of an exercising bottlenose dolphin. I co-authored a paper that detailed the behavioral training methods and equipment used for this unique research. That paper received the Outstanding Training Award from the International Marine Animal Trainers Association (IMATA) at the 1985 Annual Conference. I also pioneered the establishment of the Navy Enlisted Classification Code # 5348 (Marine Mammal Systems Operator). I compiled and edited the draft course curriculum for the Navy's first Marine Mammal Trainer and Handlers course taught at the Naval Amphibious Base (NAB) Coronado.

As an Adjunct Professor for eighteen years in the Biology Department at Point Loma Nazarene University in San Diego, I was fortunate to teach Marine Science courses, including Marine Vertebrate Zoology (with emphasis on marine mammals). Several of the students I taught and mentored became marine mammal trainers or researchers. One is on track to become a marine mammal veterinarian. They include an oceanarium assistant curator, several marine mammal trainers and marine science researchers. They currently work for the Navy, National Oceanographic and Atmospheric Administration, SeaWorld, University of California Santa Cruz Marine Mammal Lab, and Ocean Park, Hong Kong (where Stephen Leatherwood, originally at the Point Mugu Facility was the Director of the Ocean Park Conservation Foundation 1993-96).

These graduates pursuing careers in the marine sciences are proof that what began with Naval Ordnance Test Station and the Point Mugu Bioscience Facility in the 1960s, lives on today in a new generation of marine scientists and trainers.

But we're getting ahead of ourselves. Let's begin at the beginning.

INTRODUCTION

R EAR ADMIRAL ELMO R. (BUD) ZUMWALT HAD A PROBLEM.

It was September 1968. Zumwalt had just become the Commander of Naval Forces Vietnam (COMNAVFORV) and Chief of the Naval Advisory Group, U.S. Military Assistance Command Vietnam. His most recent command had been a Cruiser-Destroyer squadron, or "blue water" navy. Now he commanded a collection of "brown water" forces[1] scattered throughout Vietnam, operating in the rivers, harbors, and coastal regions.[2]

Admiral Elmo R. (Bud) Zumwalt, Chief of Naval Operations, with Rear Admiral Robert S. Salzer, Commander Naval Forces Vietnam, 1971. (U.S. Navy, 1971. Public Domain Used by permission.)

The situation was made worse by an enemy composed of both Viet Cong (VC) rebels (aka People's Liberation Armed Forces or PLAF) and North Vietnam Army regulars (NVA, aka the People's Army of Vietnam or PAVN). The VC were more independent, flexible, and operated locally (especially in the Mekong Delta) than the less flexible and more organized NVA.[3]

In his autobiography, *On Watch*, Zumwalt wrote that "Riverine warfare requires ingenuity and improvisation…. [T]he Naval Academy does not offer courses in it…. [Y]ou have to make up Riverine warfare as you go along."[4] That wasn't his biggest challenge, though. Zumwalt learned quickly that the greatest threat to US naval forces and assets in this period of the Vietnam conflict came from VC and NVA special operations forces called naval sappers.

Deadly Saboteurs

The term "sapper" comes from the French *saboteur*, which referred to "combat engineers" who laid and cleared mine fields, built bridges and performed a variety of engineering duties. French sappers in the eighteenth century sported large beards and marched in parades wearing a tan leather apron and white gloves, carrying an axe. The modern use of "sapper" has come to means a person who intentionally causes destruction of property to hinder his enemy.

In Vietnam, sappers (known in Vietnamese as *Dac Cong*, meaning "special tasks") were divided into three units. *Urban sappers* conducted intelligence gathering, terrorism, and assassinations in large urban settings. *Field sappers* trained other sappers and conducted hit-and-run raids on U.S. forces in jungles and field bases.

The third and arguably the most effective were *naval/swimmer sappers* who attacked boats, ships, barges, piers, bridges, and bases located along rivers, bays, and harbors. Swimmer sappers were thoroughly trained.[5] Underwater warfare and swimmer sapper schools were located near the Mekong Delta in the Long An and Kien Hoa provinces.[6] Swimmer sapper training differed only by the addition of swimming and water attack skills. In a way, sappers were considered between regular soldiers and guerrillas.[7]

In the summer of 1968 when Zumwalt became COMNAVFORV, swimmer sappers had increased in number, escalated their attacks, and obtained better equipment (i.e., SCUBA) and munitions (Russian Limpet mines). Water mining events tripled from forty-two in 1967 to 127 in 1968[8]. By October 1969, the NVA/VC sappers included one regiment, 47 battalions, and 31 independent companies (Battalions were divided into two to three companies with 30 to 100 sappers; companies were split into platoons with ten or more men.) The 126th NVA Swimmer Sapper Regiment with 300 men was located in the DMZ on the Cua Viet River. In South Vietnam, there were two swimmer sapper battalions, one in Bien Hoa, the other in the upper Saigon River, with from 70 to 210 men.[9]

Sappers in Vietnam

Swimmer sappers most often attacked two main areas: 1) The Naval Support Activity (NSA) and the Marine Base at Dong Ha, both on the Cua Viet River; and 2) Sea Float and the Mobile Riverine Forces (MRF) in the Cau Lon River near Nam Can in the Mekong Delta. A third site; Cam Ranh Bay (CRB), was Vietnam's largest deep-water port, and averaged more than forty supply ships each month that off-loaded ammunition and supplies. CRB was a tri-service base (Air Force, Army and Navy), with a large tri-service Ammunition Storage Facility (ASF or "ammo dump"), and was the headquarters of Operation Market Time. The ammo pier had not yet been attacked by swimmers but was a prime target and definitely in need of protection.

1) Cua Viet River Area, in Quang Tri Province, near the DMZ

Dong Ha (the capital of Quang Tri Province = CTZ-1) was about two kilometers from the DMZ, a short distance from the mouth of the Cua Viet River, on the south bank. The Marine base at Dong Ha was its main defense. Because of the turbulent waters and shifting sandbars, ships anchored outside the river mouth and supplies were off-loaded to LCMs and transported to the Naval Support Activity (NSA) inside the river mouth. From here they

Vietnam: Cua Viet River, Cam Ranh Bay, Mekong Delta (Sea Float)

Three sites (in bold) surveyed by Bill Powell, Larry Phillips and C.S. Johnson for deployment of Project Short Time. (Map image in public domain.)

were taken up the river to Dong Ha and the Advanced Tactical Support Base, CLEARWATER, near the river mouth.

Of all the Naval Facilities, Cua Viet experienced the most sapper attacks because of its proximity to the DMZ and the 126th NVA Naval/Swimmer

Sapper Regiment. These sappers continually tested the perimeter defenses at Cua Viet and Dong Ha. They also used water mines to destroy naval vessels moored to piers or transiting the river. Intelligence indicated that swimmer sappers in this area confined their activities primarily to the dark moon phases.

Along the Cua Viet River

The following are selected examples of swimmer attacks against US forces along the Cua Viet River between Dong Ha and the Naval Support Activity at the mouth of the river.[10]

On 28 April 1968, a river patrol boat spotted two swimmers in the river but they escaped. A week later (5 May 1968) an NVA swimmer was captured at Dong Ha and interrogated. He revealed a plan for swimmer sappers to mine and sink a large supply ship just east of Dong Ha, in a narrow part of the river. Land forces would then come from the DMZ, cross where the ship was to be sunk, and attack Dong Ha. The sunken ship would block the river and prevent re-supplying the Marines in Dong Ha. The next day, a regiment of NVA, not knowing the sapper plan had failed, crossed the DMZ, expecting to easily cross the river and take Dong Ha. Instead, they were caught off guard and repelled by US and RVN forces at Dai Do Village. The incident demonstrated the high value of capturing swimmer sappers alive for interrogation.[11]

On 21 February 1969, NVA swimmer sappers mined LCM-6 "Mike" boats moored at the Advanced Tactical Support Base, CLEARWATER, near the mouth of the Cua Viet River. Three separate explosions sunk an LCM-6 and caused moderate hull damage to three LCM- 8s. EOD divers determined all three explosions were from BPM-2, Soviet-made limpet mines (with a 6 pound 10 ounce charge) probably placed by NVA sappers. VC swimmers preferred using larger (30-40 pound) charges and rarely used limpet mines.[12]

Three weeks later on 15 March 1969, swimmer sappers blew up a railroad bridge. The CK-2 Naval Sapper Company reportedly was directed to destroy this I Corps Bridge before the end of March. Five days later, on 20 March 1969, a "Mike" boat hit an underwater mine while transiting the Cua Viet River. Luckily there were no casualties or damage.[13]

The next day, 21 March 1969, a river patrol boat on the Cua Dai River saw a large explosion from a command detonated mine just off its starboard. Again, luckily, there were no casualties or damage.[14]

In July 1970, a water mine exploded in the Cua Viet River, sinking a civilian water taxi and killing an estimated thirty to fifty Vietnamese.[15]

2) The Mobile Riverine Force in the Mekong Delta and Sea Float

Viet Cong sappers in the Mekong ("9 Dragons") Delta were isolated from major sapper commands in South Vietnam but nevertheless were extremely effective. Their supplies came mainly from North Vietnam via the Ho Chi Minh trail, and aided them in gaining unchallenged control of the Ca Mau peninsula. As the new COMNAVFORV, Zumwalt was determined to disrupt their supply line and seriously reduce their effectiveness in the Delta.

Building and defending a shore base in this region in the summer of 1968 was impossible. Zumwalt's Assistant Chief of Staff for Operations, CDR "Dick" Nicholson, proposed using an array of pontoon barges to establish a floating Mobile Advanced Tactical Support Base (MATSB) in the Cua Lon River. Then, after establishing an effective presence in this region, an Advanced Tactical Support Base (ASTB) could be built nearby on the north bank of the river. This plan became "Operation Sea Float/Solid Anchor" (CTG 116.1).[16]

Attacks before Sea Float

The following are selected examples of swimmer attacks before Sea Float was established, some were very deadly.[17]

At 0323, 1 November 1968, VC swimmers attached two large mines (150-500 lbs) to the hull of the USS WESTCHESTER COUNTY (LST-1167) anchored in the My Tho River. The explosion killed twenty-five and wounded twenty-seven, with four missing. The ship was severely damaged, along with two helicopters and three assault craft. This was the U.S. Navy's greatest loss of personnel in a single action.[18]

Two weeks later, on 15 November 1968, swimmers attacked a light salvage lift craft (YLLC-4) anchored with the Mobile Riverine Force (MRF) in the Ham Luong River near the entrance to the Ben Tre River. Two explosions occurred only seconds apart that immediately sunk the ship, stern first. Two sailors were killed and thirteen wounded. The ship was badly damaged and the hull became a hazard to navigation. On 26 November 1968, a Harbor Clearance unit destroyed the hull with explosives.[19]

Sea Float Defenses

The following are selected examples of swimmer attacks after Sea Float was established.

Sea Float began on 25 June 1969, when eleven pontoon barges were tied together and anchored in the Cau Lon River, with 6-9 knot tidal currents. Sea Float was home to 150 personnel who fed and supported approximately 700 men. These included a River

Sea Float anchored in middle of Cua Lon River. (Photo Courtesy of John Yeoman.)

Assault Group, a Beach Jumper unit, three SEAL platoons, one UDT detachment, two SeaWolf attack helicopters, SEAL support craft, and a wide assortment of US and VNN Riverine craft. Defensive capabilities included four US Navy snipers who provided early warning of movements along the river banks. The barges had multiple M-60 gun mounts around the periphery with 81 mm motors at each corner.[20]

Even with these defenses, Nicholson's plan was made difficult by naval/swimmer sappers who attacked Sea Float barges and various Riverine water craft moored or anchored nearby. To deter them, several anti-swimmer methods were tried, including nets, sonar and "water dogs".

Sea Float barges and some riverine craft used anti-swimmer nets which occasionally entangled water mines delivered by swimmer sappers and were then cleared or neutralized by EOD divers.

Zumwalt tested several anti-swimmer systems at Sea Float. One used a Sonar mounted on an LCM-6 and operated by a 1st Class Sonarman. This system proved unsuccessful and was canceled. He also tried water dogs, trained to detect the exhaled breath of swimmers. The dogs were patrolled around Sea Float on nineteen-foot outboard boats, but due to exhaust fumes and "other factors", the dogs never detected a swimmer.

A third system, developed at the Naval Mine Defense Laboratory (MDL), Panama City, Florida was operated by humans who used an array of sonabuoys and a mortar. It was field-tested but demanded extreme vigilance and concentration during all night operations. More importantly, it only detected targets; it could not classify them (i.e., discriminate between swimmers, sharks, turtles, logs, etc). Additionally, firing mortars on unconfirmed targets, at close range was dangerous and would most likely exclude any possibility of interrogating the sapper.

Meanwhile, a SECRET fourth system was being developed at the Naval Undersea Center's Hawaii Laboratory that used dolphins to detect and mark swimmers. But its time had not yet arrived.

So the most effective swimmer countermeasure at Sea Float remained having sentries randomly throwing concussion grenades into the water, all night. Obviously the off-duty personnel did not sleep well.

Attacks on Sea Float

At 2050, 21 April 1970, sentries on Sea Float saw air bubbles at regular intervals and began dropping concussion grenades until the bubbles ceased. Later that night at 0237, a sentry saw a swimmer approaching Sea Float's eastern mooring buoy and immediately threw grenades into the water. Other sentries fired at the swimmer and General Quarters was sounded. Sentries at the M-60 mounts saw two more swimmers near the Sea Float fuel barge and fired until the swimmers disappeared. Grenades were dropped randomly for forty-five minutes, then stopped so EOD divers could check mooring chains and barges for charges/mines. None were found.

The next day, two bodies were found downstream, one shot in the head, the other shot in the arm and apparently drowned. These swimmers were carrying sealed waterproof bags with explosives, timing pencils, and detonation material but fortunately didn't have time to use them. A day later, a third body was found, shot in the head with an M-60 round. This swimmer had a waterproof bag with 250 quarter-pound blocks (i.e., 100 pounds) of TNT, ten pounds of plastic explosives and twenty-four blasting caps.

Up to then, Sea Float had gone 9 months (June 1969-April 1970) without a confirmed swimmer attack. Now, apparently, VC swimmers were attempting to inflict major damage to Zumwalt's personal project. Ordnance specialists informed him that the swimmers had sufficient explosives to completely sink Sea Float. So in his message congratulating Sea Float's crew for a job well done, Zumwalt included this: "The threat from swimmer sappers is ever present and the highest possible degree of readiness to defend from such a threat is mandatory." Sea Float's commander now instructed his sentries to randomly drop grenades every night.[21]

At 2000, 30 July 1970, the VNN Gunship LSSL- 225, anchored 1,000 yards east-northeast of Sea Float, was attacked by swimmer sappers using a floating mine. The ship flooded quickly, turned upside down and sunk in five minutes, killing 28 Vietnamese sailors, mostly those below decks. The ship was never salvaged and was left where it had sunk in the Cau Lon River.[22]

On 23 August 1970, the USS-GALLOP (PG-85) was attacked by a three-man team of VC swimmer sappers while anchored just west of Sea Float. A roving patrol skimmer detected the three swimmers and forced them to the surface with concussion grenades. One swimmer was shot by a guard on the GALLOP; the other two disappeared below the surface after being grenaded several times. The ship got underway while the area was saturated with grenades. A few days later, bodies of two swimmers were recovered nearby but not the one that was shot.[23]

In mid-September 1970, Sea Float transitioned to a land-based Advanced Tactical Support Base (ASTB), Solid Anchor, as originally planned. Later on 1 April, 1971, as part of Nixon's Vietnamization plan, Solid Anchor was turned over to the RVN.

Continued Attacks on Mobile Riverine Forces

At 0520, 3 October 1970, the VNN LSSL-226 sunk in only five minutes in the Co Chien River when a floating mine with a timing device blew a hole in its port side. The mine had been attached to the anchor chain by a swimmer who came and went with the current. There were no deaths, but two VNN were wounded and one missing.

At 0155, 6 October 1970, the Advanced Tactical Support Base (ATSB) known as Breezy Cove, situated at the mouth of the Ong Doc River, was attacked by swimmer sappers who successfully sunk two PBRs. PBR-36 was sitting with its bow on the beach and sunk immediately. PBR-37 was next to it and got underway, but not in time. A charge had already been placed on it and exploded when they pulled away. There were no survivors from either PBR.[24]

Two weeks later on 20 October, the Breezy Cove ATSB was completely destroyed by rockets and mortars. Breezy Cove was never rebuilt at the original site. However, a few weeks later old Sea Float barges were towed in and anchored at a new site a few miles up the river.[25]

3) Cam Ranh Bay (Tri-Service Base)

The third major target of sappers was CRB, the largest deep water harbor in Vietnam.[26] Located on the east coast of Vietnam in the II Corp military region, the tri-service (Air Force, Army and Navy) base occupied thirty-nine square miles (18 X 5.5 miles) with a huge perimeter, much of it ocean shoreline. Its deep-water piers had Sea-Land ships off-loading ordnance and supplies almost around the clock.[27] This base was considered a strategic site and was the headquarters for Operation Market Time. It should be noted that Swimmer Sapper Company (K-93) with an estimated seven men was located just north of Cam Ranh Bay.

In 1971, the base population included 9,600 Army, 7,000 Air Force, 460 Navy and 13,000 Vietnamese who came through the Ma Ca Village (Cam Ranh Ville) checkpoint. An average of 40 ships/month entered the harbor and unloaded 28,000 short tons and 29 million gallons of POL. A short distance from the pier was a large ammo dump with several large petroleum/oil/lubricant (POL) storage tanks. Army convoys averaged 10 long hauls and 60 short hauls per month to resupply U.S. forces.

During October 1970, CRB harbor patrol boats operating in what was called Operation Stable Door, inspected a total of 1,310 watercrafts, boarded 582 and detained 58 persons in 52 of the watercraft.

On 23 May 1969, field sappers blew up six POL tanks that burned for two weeks. At 0100, 11 August 1969, 107mm rockets hit the Air Base while field sappers from the ocean side came through the perimeter fence on the north end of the base at the 6th Convalescent Center. They ran through the compound tossing satchel charges into nineteen of the ninety-four convalescent buildings that housed injured patients and unarmed personnel. Eighty-nine personnel were wounded and two died from these blasts. Obviously such a cheap shot, even during a war, did not sit well with the patients and medical personnel.[26]

On 1 April 1970, field sappers attacked and destroyed three POL storage tanks. Military Police responded and searched but could not find the sappers.

At 0130, 12 June 1970, the Naval Air Facility (NAF) was first attacked by rockets and mortars and then by NVA Field Sappers with AK-47s, RPGs and satchel charges. The sappers blasted through the main gate and fired an RPG into the guard tower killing a sentry. One sapper threw a satchel charge into the diesel generator, knocking out power to the base. Another ran into an airplane hangar and blew up the "head" and an administration office. Other sappers threw charges into revetments that protected parked aircraft. Security forces killed two sappers, wounded one and captured one, but most of the sappers escaped though concertina wire into the adjacent Ma Ca Village.[26]

At 0226, 26 August 1971, while the Short Time dolphins were guarding the ammo pier, field sappers again came from the ocean side and attacked the tri-service ammo dump with satchel charges and rockets. The sappers exited the base on the ocean side, just as they came. Munitions of all types exploded and burned for two days, destroying a total of 6,000 tons of ordnance valued at the time at more than US $10 million.[26]

Zumwalt's Solution

Clearly Zumwalt desperately needed an efficient and effective anti-swimmer system.

On a trip through Hawaii, Zumwalt visited CINCPACFLT and inquired about the status of a Navy dolphin system he had heard about that could detect, classify and mark swimmers. He was told by a staff officer that it was not ready yet.

The truth is that the dolphin swimmer defense system, that was the focus of ONR's Advanced Marine Biological Systems program, was virtually ready seven months before Sea Float was attacked — in December 1969.

How it was developed, shelved, resurfaced, and ultimately deployed is the story of this book.

I

EARLY YEARS AT POINT MUGU

(1960-1967)

1

The Navy's First Dolphins: NOTS, China Lake and NMC Point Mugu (1960-1964)

I N A WAY, THE STORY OF DEFENDER DOLPHINS BEGINS in a remote dry lake bed in the Mojave Desert, 130 miles from any ocean. That's where William B. McLean served as Technical Director of Naval Ordnance Test Station (NOTS), China Lake, California.

McLean was a brilliant civilian physicist who held forty-nine patents and developed the famous heat-seeking air-to-air Sidewinder missile. He also was very interested in marine mammals. That's how he came to be the driving force behind the purchase of Notty, the Navy's first dolphin.

(McLean's intense focus on marine mammals was well known to NOTS personnel. For several years at Christmas time in early 1960s, McLean drove around the residential areas with a porpoise float on the truck bed, blasting a recording, "Ho! Ho! Ho! This is Notty, the red-nosed porpoise!")[1]

Dr. Bill McLean, NOTS, China Lake, California, the creative genius who foresaw that marine mammals were a new frontier for the U.S. Navy.

On the Pacific Coast, near Oxnard, NOTS had formed a collaboration with the Point Mugu Naval Missile Center (NMC). This is where the center of the Navy's marine mammal research would begin in the summer of 1962. But Notty came a few years prior. She was a Pacific white-sided dolphin (*Lagenorhyncus obliquidens*) purchased in 1960 from the Marineland of Pacific (MOP) in Palos Verdes, California. She was trained for a hydrodynamics study conducted by Thomas G. Lang in the Convair Laboratory tow tank in San Diego, California. NOTS contracted Ralph Penner, a trainer at MOP, to work with Notty. This made Penner the first civilian marine mammal trainer for the Navy. At the conclusion of the hydrodynamic tests, Notty was taken to MOP because the Navy didn't yet have any holding facilities. Here she was maintained and studied extensively until she died in December 1961.

Ralph Penner, the Navy's first marine mammal trainer, with Notty, NOTS's first dolphin, 1961. *(U.S. Navy. Used by permission.)*

Back at Point Mugu in November of 1961 it became known that NMC planned to fill a portion of Mugu Lagoon for a rifle range. Local citizens were concerned that the Navy was not protecting the region's biological communities. A small group of Navy scientists headed by LCDR James Berrian, in the

Life Sciences Department at NMC, supported these citizens. That summer, the Navy responded by establishing a Marine Bioscience Division at Point Mugu and contracted two highly regarded marine scientists, Drs. George and Nellie McGinitie, authors of *The Natural History of Marine Animals*, to survey and catalogue the lagoon's marine life.

The Navy assigned two divers, Technical Device (TD) Petty Officers, Bill Scronce and Marty Conboy, (and later Dave Spong) to collect specimens for the McGinities. Scronce and Conboy knew very little about identifying marine organisms. To help them, every morning the McGinities showed them color photos of the organisms they wanted collected. After a few questions, Scronce and Conboy would get their dive gear and spend the day diving and looking for the target specimens. (They did not know it at the time, but they would become the Navy's first military marine mammal trainers.)

The Right Species of Dolphins

After the Notty study in San Diego, McLean made Lang the coordinator of his NOTS Cetacean Research Program. McLean wanted to continue

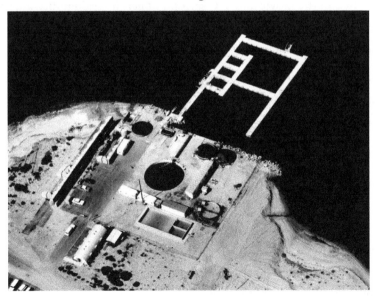

An aerial view of the Point Mugu Naval Missile Center, where the center of the Navy's marine mammal research would begin in 1962. *(U.S. Navy. Used by permission.)*

studying dolphin hydrodynamics, communication, and man-dolphin applications. He knew the Navy needed holding facilities if it was to properly study marine mammals. In 1962 he funded the construction of a concrete pool to house dolphins at the Point Mugu Bioscience Facility. It was a circular concrete tank fifty feet in diameter and eight feet deep. He also donated an old Quonset hut, two old walk-in freezers, and two small trailers.

The next month the Navy purchased three Pacific white-sided dolphins from a fisherman in Santa Monica. After being placed in the pool, they each died over a short period of time from unknown causes.

What scientists came to learn was that white-sided dolphins are pelagic and swim constantly in the open ocean; thus they do not adapt well to enclosed tanks. Bottlenose dolphins (*Tursiops truncatus*), however, are not pelagic; they inhabit bays, coastal, and estuarine environments and do not swim constantly. This species of dolphins adapts very well to proper sized enclosures, and can tolerate human activities and their pollutants. The bottlenose dolphin was the star performer in early US ocean parks, such as Pacific Ocean Park, Marine Studios, Coney Island, and Marineland of the Pacific, and was used in the movie and TV series, *Flipper*. Its trainability, adaptability to various environments, and exceptional echolocation abilities made it the best species for most Navy applications.

That discovery, and the elementary framework of a marine mammal program, meant the Navy's dolphin military research was now underway.

ABE Connection

In September 1962, the Marine Bioscience Division acquired two Atlantic bottlenose dolphins that had been captured off Gulfport, Mississippi. The Point Mugu holding tanks were still not yet ready, so the dolphins had to be temporarily kept at POP. Sam, Bill, and Marty drove daily to POP to study their two animals, named Dot and Dash, and to learn what they could about behavioral conditioning from Wally and Mo.

Also in 1962, Bill McLean hired Bob Bailey to be the Cetacean Research Project's first Director of Training at Point Mugu. Bailey, a UCLA graduate, was a self-taught animal trainer. Bob applied what he'd learned about the scientific principles of operant conditioning from the works of B. F. Skinner, and Keller and Marian Breland. He had met the Brelands and knew about their company, Animal Behavior Enterprises (ABE) in Hot Springs, Arkansas.

The Brelands were well known for teaching operant conditioning techniques to perspective animal trainers. They had a simple method using a clicker, as a "bridge", to condition chickens and other animals. McLean had Kent Burgess of ABE come to NOTS and give a presentation. He was significantly impressed and arranged for Burgess and Keller Breland to teach Wally, Marty, Bill, and Bailey about operant conditioning. They packed up their chickens and acoustic clickers and came to Point Mugu. This was the beginning of an important relationship with ABE.

Now They Had Five Dolphins

Dr. Clint Maag, the head of the Life Sciences Department at Point Mugu, needed someone with marine mammal experience to supervise and manage his small pioneering group of marine mammal researchers. Clint was told by the Office of Naval Research that Forrest Glenn (Woody) Wood, Jr., the general curator at Marineland of Florida, was the person for this job. To this day Marineland (originally, Marine Studios founded in 1938) near St. Augustine, Florida, remains the world's oldest continuously operating oceanarium. In 1963, Clint invited Woody to visit the Point Mugu facility and consider being hired.

After his visit, Woody returned to Marineland and arranged to have three Atlantic bottlenose dolphins sold to the Point Mugu Marine Bioscience Division. Also in 1963, McLean moved NOTS' Cetacean Research program, headed by Tom Lang, to the Point Mugu Naval Missile Center's Marine Bioscience Division.[2]

To learn more about dolphins and how to transport them, Bill, Marty, Bob and the newly hired veterinarian Sam Ridgway (see sidebar, "How to Become a Marine Mammal Veterinarian") flew to Marineland for an in-depth tour and to learn how to transport dolphins. With this knowledge, they transported their three new dolphins back to Point Mugu in a Navy cargo plane. They now had five dolphins to train, care for, and study.

In June 1963, Woody arrived at Point Mugu to work as a civil servant. Woody's job was to manage, three biologists, two engineers, one veterinarian (Ridgway), and six military personnel. He also had a small group of researchers (two full-time and six part-time), including Bill Evans, a UCLA graduate student, and Tom Lang, the NOTS scientist, who came from NOTS Pasadena.

In early 1964, Bill Powell arrived from NOTS, at McLean's insistence, to solve administrative issues that interfered with research. (See Chapter 3 sidebar, "The Management Genius of Point Mugu.") Bill began by hiring a secretary to reduce the scientist's paperwork load. After a few other procedural changes, the Bioscience Facility was soon running smoothly however, funding was limited and always a distracting issue.

Meanwhile, Bob Bailey was focused on using operant conditioning technology to train a dolphin to swim in the open ocean under trainer control — a requisite step to Navy applications using marine mammals.

Ridgway had become very interested in this type of animal research, and Hall knew he needed a full-time veterinarian because the last three Navy dolphins had died soon after being purchased. When a fourth dolphin died, Hall asked Ridgway to come to Point Mugu and perform the necropsy. Ridgway had never seen the insides of a dolphin but said he'd "be glad to give it a try". His experience with other animals equipped him to determine that the dolphin had died of pneumonia.

A week later in a meeting with Ridgway and several scientists, Hall announced that he wanted to hire Ridgway as a full-time veterinarian. This was just what Ridgway had hoped for, but he was a bit surprised by the way Hall had presented it to the scientists Ridgway would be working with.

Hall said he would immediately begin working to make the appointment happen, and in the meantime, Ridgway should learn all he could about caring for dolphins. Hall told him to go visit the people at Pacific Ocean Park (POP) in Santa Monica.

HOW TO BECOME THE WORLD'S FIRST MARINE MAMMAL VETERINARIAN

Not far from the Point Mugu NMC was Oxnard Air Force Base in Camarillo, California. Captain Sam H. Ridgway, DVM, had been the base veterinarian there since 1960. He was scheduled to complete his active duty obligation in October 1962. While at Oxnard AFB, Ridgway had occasionally worked with the research animals at Point Mugu. Up to this point, the NOTS dolphins had been under the care of CDR Lee Hall, an aviation medicine MD who also was responsible for the Navy scientists who studied them.

Captain Sam H. Ridgway, DVM, prior to leaving the US Air Force, 1962. Ridgway was the Navy's first full-time marine mammal veterinarian and an early employee of what later became the Navy's Marine Mammal Program. *(Courtesy of Sam H. Ridgway.)*

This was the real beginning of marine mammal education for not only Ridgway but also the two navy divers, TD Petty Officers Bill Scronce and Marty Conboy. Wally Ross and Morris ("Mo") F. Wintermantel, the trainers at POP, were more than happy to provide them valuable training. Ross and Wintermantel continued to contribute significantly during the nascent years of the Navy's marine mammal program.

In October 1962, when Ridgway's military obligation ended, CDR Hall hired him to be the Naval Missile Center's Animal Health Officer. Ridgway did not know it then, but this made him the very first full-time marine mammal veterinarian, and an early employee of what later became the Navy's Marine Mammal Program.

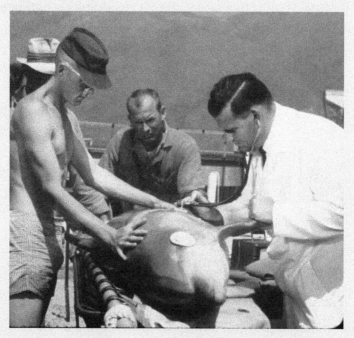

At Point Mugu, Sam H. Ridgway (right) examines Dash (called Maui after being moved to Hawaii). Marty Conboy (left) and Mo Wintermantel observe. *(Courtesy of Sam H. Ridgway, 1963-64.)*

2

The Year of Open-Ocean Released Marine Mammals (1964)

I N MARCH 1964, SAM RIDGWAY AND FORREST GLEN (Woody) Wood, Jr., learned that Pacific Ocean Park (POP) was closing, and veteran trainers Wally Ross and Mo Wintermantel both needed jobs. They immediately hired them.

POP also had sold off all its animals, except one. He was a scarred, emaciated, yet feisty and aggressive male dolphin called Tuf Guy, later known as Tuffy, and he was the last animal left because no one wanted him. Yet Mo urged Sam to buy him. Since POP wanted only $150, Sam agreed. Woody arranged for the purchase, trading electronic equipment for the dolphin.

Tuffy was taken to Point Mugu, where he acted out his name. That summer a UCLA biology student, Debbie Duffield, worked as Sam's research assistant. During that summer she gradually gained Tuffy's confidence and tamed him. Debbie began by standing in his enclosure and rewarding him with fish for incremental increases in calm behavior. At the end of the summer, Wally Ross took over training Tuffy.

Tuffy would go on to set records, foster many scientific discoveries about dolphin physiology, and even become the star of Navy movies. But no one knew that then.

Roxie Returns

Meanwhile, Bailey was focused on training marine mammals to swim in the open ocean and return to their trainer.

During the summer of 1964, Bill Evans, a doctoral student at UCLA, came to Point Mugu and brought with him Roxie, his California sea lion (*Zalophus califorianus*). Evans was also interested in open-ocean releasing marine mammals. He and Wally began training Roxie to recover objects in her pen, the lagoon, and ultimately in open ocean.

In early August 1964, Roxie became the first marine mammal in captivity to be released into the ocean and return. At a command, she dove to 120 feet off Anacapa Island, one of the Channel Islands. Later she dove to 240 feet, which seemed to approach her dive limit.

What was at stake? To develop marine mammal systems for Navy applications, many of which had been suggested by John Lilly in 1961 in his ground-breaking work, *Man and Dolphin*[1], one had to demonstrate that dolphins and pinnipeds could be released into the open ocean and reliably return to their trainer. Open-ocean release was critical.

Buzz and Buzz-Buzz

Earlier in October 1963, four Atlantic bottlenose dolphins were collected off Gulfport, Mississippi. Buzz and Buzz-Buzz and two others were taken directly to Animal Behavior Enterprises (ABE) in Hot Springs, Arkansas, for training, feeding, and behavioral studies. In February 1964, Buzz-Buzz (a female) and the other three dolphins were transported from ABE to Point Mugu.

Here Buzz-Buzz was trained by Bailey to wear a harness, pinger recall, tow a small boat, and go through pen gates. In April 1964 she worked in a netted-off portion of the Mugu Lagoon and gradually increased her pinger recall distance to more than 100 meters (300 feet). By June her recall distance had tripled up to 300 meters (900 feet).She had also been trained to enter a stretcher so she could be lifted from the water and transported in a truck.

On 13 August 1964, after five months of training, Bob Bailey transported Buzz-Buzz to Port Hueneme, California. There, he and Buzz-Buzz performed the first open-ocean release of a Navy dolphin.

Bob Bailey, with Buzz-Buzz, the first dolphin ever to be released into the open ocean and return. This achievement in 1964 was a critical point in the development of marine mammal systems. *(Courtesy of Bob Bailey, 1964.)*

Bailey, who much later became the owner of Animal Behavior Enterprise, was asked in an interview to describe his favorite training moment. "Every time you release an animal, it could go somewhere else. In spite of [having] 99.999 percent success, that next release could result in an animal running, flying, or swimming away," he said. "That is 100 percent failure. If you have never released and recovered a trained wild animal, you cannot fully comprehend the feeling."[2]

The accomplishment came *only ten days* before Ken Norris, at the Oceanic Institute, released a Pacific bottlenose dolphin (*Tursiops gilli*) named Keiki on 28 August in Kaneohe Bay, Oahu.

This was a crucial point in the future development of marine mammal systems. Now the sky was the limit, so to speak, for mankind's use of dolphins and sea lions in the open sea.

"WE'VE GOT FLIPPER!"

While the Navy was studying marine mammal capabilities and training them for open-ocean releases at Point Mugu, Ricou Browning was in Florida training a dolphin in similar ways, but for vastly different goals.

Ricou was creator, co-author, and producer of the screenplay for the hit movie and TV series, *Flipper*.[1] He and his partner, Ivan Tors, needed a dolphin to play the part, and had been turned down by several marine aquariums.

The entrepreneurs learned of a fisherman and dolphin catcher named Milton Santini who kept a pet dolphin, Mitzi, in a lagoon near his home at Grassy Key, Florida. When Santini captured wild dolphins for aquariums, he would release them into the lagoon with Mitzi. The wild dolphins would observe her eating the dead fish he tossed to her and soon they would begin doing the same. (Getting wild dolphins to shift from eating live to dead fish is not easy and takes time.)

Ricou and Ivan drove to Grassy Key and told Santini they were looking for a dolphin for a movie project. Without hesitation, Milton said, "She's over there. Go take a look at her."

They walked to Santini's lagoon. Ricou got into the shallow water and began wading out. When he got about chest deep, Mitzi swam around him and then stuck her rostrum (nose) under his arm.

Ricou looked up at Ivan, who was standing on the lagoon's small dock, and said, "We've got Flipper!"

The rest is history. Ricou and his son, Ricou Jr., began training Mitzi (now aka Flipper) in May, 1962 for two months before filming the first *Flipper* feature movie. Mitzi learned to retrieve objects both above and underwater, and to work between trainers located above or underwater. She was also trained to tow a boy holding her dorsal fin and to perform various tricks. Later in the summer of 1962, Mitzi was taken to Nassau, Bahamas, for more training and to perform in a large enclosure where the movie *Flipper* was filmed.[2] The original *Flipper* movie was not released until August 1963.

Ricou's son doubled[3] all the underwater scenes for the movie's boy actor, Luke Halpin. Most importantly, Mitzi was trained to perform her tasks in the presence of a variety of detracting objects, sights and sounds (for example, cameras running, divers, people swimming, light reflectors, and men hammering).

When asked where he learned about animal training, Ricou said, "I had visited several marine aquariums and watched trainers throw fish to dolphins when they performed a trick correctly, so that's what I did."

Milton Santini, the Florida Keys fisherman who captured all the Short Time dolphins, plays with Mitzi, who appeared in the movie, Flipper. *(Courtesy of Bob Bailey, 1962.)*

3

Red Eye Studies:
The Proof-of-Concept of Swimmer Detection
by Navy Dolphins
(1965-67)

I N JULY 1965, TUFFY WAS INVITED TO PARTICIPATE IN SeaLab II scheduled for September off La Jolla, California. For six weeks he trained to carry tools and rescue lost divers near the SeaLab habitat, located on the bottom at 205 feet in the underwater La Jolla Canyon. CAPT George Bond, from the Mine Defense Lab in Panama City, Florida, was the Dive Medical Officer for SeaLab II. He was quite impressed with Tuffy's performance with divers, and suggested to Sam Ridgway that it might be worth exploring the use of his dolphins in other, "less friendly" tasks.

"Dolphin Mail": The envelope that held a letter to Bill Quigley in Panama City, Florida, written by aquanaut Wally Jenkins while 200 feet undersea in SEALAB II. Tuffy delivered the mail to the surface for "regular delivery". This was the first occasion of a dolphin being used for a Navy operation. *(Courtesy of Bill Quigley, 1965.)*

Bond said he would help Sam get funding to conduct such studies.[1] Sam received the special funding in early 1966 and hired Blair Irvine to train a dolphin named Red Eye. The aim of the project was to prove that a dolphin could be trained to search for, detect, and report the presence of a human swimmer.

Blair trained Red Eye to swim a triangular route marked with buoys and return to the pen and push a response paddle, telling Blair if he had detected a swimmer. To monitor Red Eye's search, Blair attached small flags to each of the buoys. Red Eye was to bump each buoy as he swam past each of them along the triangular course. This made the flag wiggle so Blair knew Red Eye was swimming the proper course.

Blair's work with Red Eye was successful and history-making. This was the first proof-of-concept conducted by a US Navy research laboratory.

Next, Red Eye and two other dolphins were flown to the Navy's Mine Defense Laboratory in Panama City, where CAPT Bond was assigned.[2] Here trainers tested the dolphins' ability to detect both SCUBA and closed-circuit divers. Here also, researchers learned how far dolphins could detect divers — surprising the scientists and especially the Navy divers involved.

The next year, in March 1967, Sam hired Don McSheehy, a civil servant, to work at the Point Mugu Facility. Don had been the Director of Animal Training at the Aquatarium in St. Petersburg, Florida, for several years and had met Sam during a visit there. Don's first task was to train a new dolphin, Rounder, for open-ocean release. Rounder soon became Point Mugu's fourth open-ocean control dolphin. Don also trained a Navy dolphin to attach a package to the driveshaft or hull of a sampan as part of Sam's military applications project.

In a few months, January 1968, Don would move to Hawaii to become the fourth full-time employee at the NUC Hawaii Laboratory and, later, the head trainer for Project Short Time.

THE MANAGEMENT GENIUS OF POINT MUGU

With his program management and communication skills, Bill A. Powell was unquestionably the individual primarily responsible for the initial and lasting success of the Navy's Marine Mammal Program. He had an innate ability to solve personality conflicts and motivate people to perform well, regardless of their circumstances. His knowledge and application of psychology made those who worked with him never fully realize what they agreed to do, until after he had left the conversation. He was the master of "tact" (i.e., when someone tells you something and you don't fully realize what they said until you are out of earshot).

Bill grew up in the Los Angeles area where he became an avid hotrod fan and an excellent mechanic. After high school he decided to study to become a musician. After a year, he realized that was no way to make a living and applied to the US Foreign Service. He was assigned to Mogadishu, Somalia, and then Paris. He left the Foreign Service to return to Los Angeles State College and earn a bachelor's degree in Political Science.

After graduating, he was hired by NOTS China Lake and worked for Thomas (Tom) Milburn, a social psychologist who headed the Behavioral Sciences Group. In late 1963, NOTS Technical Director, Bill McLean, asked Powell to go visit the Point Mugu Bioscience Division and evaluate their management structure. McLean was committed to the NOTS marine mammal research and wanted NOTS studies to proceed efficiently.

At that time Point Mugu Naval Missile Center (NMC) Bioscience Division had three biologists/trainers, seven military personnel (including two Navy divers/trainers), and a civilian veterinarian, who were "managed" by a scientist, F.G. Wood (Woody). In addition, NOTS had two full-time researchers, six part-time researchers, and Bob Bailey as Director of Training — all "managed" by Tom Lang who made frequent visits from NOTS Pasadena Lab. To put it kindly, this arrangement was not working well.

Powell took little time in recognizing the problems. In his report to McLean, Powell recommended he assign a resident manager of equal GS grade to Woody and Lang, and hire a secretary. This way the scientists could focus on research and stop wasting time typing memos and performing time-consuming routine paperwork.

McLean was impressed. A few days later, in early 1964 he called Powell to his office and offered him the job of managing NOTS/NMC Cetacean Research Project at Point Mugu. Powell was quick to point out that he was only a GS-11 and Woody and Lang were GS-13s.

Powell recalls that McLean, a person who didn't let rules hinder progress, told Powell to come with him to the Personnel Department, adding, "I'll make you a GS-13." When Powell said that was impossible, McLean replied, "I'm the TD of this laboratory. I can do what I want."

Alas, the Head of Personnel confirmed that McLean could not get his way this time, because Powell did not yet have enough time-in-grade. McLean was not happy, and insisted Powell go to Point Mugu anyway and implement his recommendations, equal GS level or not.

4

The Vietnam Connection: Zumwalt Seeks Solutions from NOTS (1967)

THE INDUSTIAL MEDICAL OFFICER WHO SERVED AT NOTS China Lake from 1965 to 1973 was a physician named Elmo R. Zumwalt, Sr. Dr. Zumwalt and his wife, Doris, were close friends with NOTS Technical Director Bill McLean and his wife, LaV.

Dr. Zumwalt happened to have a son in the US Navy. One could say he was pretty high ranking. From August 1966 to August 1968, Rear Admiral Elmo R. (Bud) Zumwalt, Jr., was the Director of Chief of Naval Operations Systems Analysis Group. He also was Deputy Scientific Officer to the Center for Naval Analysis. His job required him to stay informed of problems the Navy had worldwide. He was in a position to know which labs were most successful in conducting research to solve these problems, including a pioneering marine mammal program like the one connected to McLean. The Navy had a problem that needed an innovative solution.

Somehow, the Zumwalt Sr.-McLean friendship resulted in Admiral Zumwalt Jr. sending a classified personal message to McLean, requesting help in solving the Vietnam swimmer sapper problem. (See the Introduction.) Apparently comprehending the potential of the dolphin project, Zumwalt asked McLean to go visit several sites in Vietnam and bring him back some recommendations.

Unfortunately, McLean was scheduled for cataract surgery. He sent Bill Powell and a sonar engineer in his place.

Powell recalls that most of the sites he visited in Vietnam had fast-moving water, which would make it difficult for dolphins to work properly. In his report to McLean, Powell suggested that perhaps a dolphin could be trained to detect swimmers from some sort of enclosure or stationary pen.

Powell never heard what Rear Admiral Zumwalt did after McLean sent him his suggestions.

"PORPOISE TORPEDOS"

Earlier in 1966, Bill Powell and Bill Evans had conducted research and presented findings on the dolphin's exceptional echolocation abilities. In April of that year, their study, "Discrimination of Different Metallic Plates by an Echolocating Porpoise", was presented at a Marine Science Symposium of the American Institute of Aeronautics and Astronautics.

The research, which was later published in the journal, *Animal Sonar Systems—Biology and Bionics, Vol. I, 1967,* led to wild speculation by the news media about the "Navy Training Kamikaze Dolphins".

Newspapers had a field day. Headlines ranged from the relatively mild "Navy Scientists Have Taught Porpoises to Detect Metal" and "Porpoises Learn Tricks for War", to the outrageous "Porpoise Torpedos"; "Porpoises to Sniff Out Submarines"; "Bomb-Laden Porpoises Possible Navy Weapon"; and "Armed Porpoises: New Secret Weapon?" and more.

Powell has shown me a scrapbook full of these wildly speculating newspaper headlines. It would be funny except too many people blindly believe this. Unfortunately, the media's interpretation of the results from a well-conducted scientific study, has taken on a life of its own and keeps popping up in the press.

5

Much Ado about an ADO and ADP: Finding Funding (Spring-Fall 1967)

I N THE SPRING OF 1967, NAVY SCIENTISTS AT THE POINT Mugu facility needed to expand their pioneering marine mammal research programs. This would require a move to warmer waters.

Until then they had survived with small, $30-$50k independent research (IR) studies that had not required trainers to spend long hours in the cold Pacific. The results of these small initial training studies were so promising that they believed it was time to obtain more reliable, long-term funding. They wanted a marine mammal program that could develop new capabilities for the Navy not attainable with other technologies. Their first step was for the program leaders, Bill Powell and Forrest G. Wood ("Woody") to go to Washington DC for advice from one of their sponsors, Sam Rothman.

Rothman was the Head of Exploratory Development (aka 6.2) Research at Naval Materiel Command (NAVMAT). Bill and Woody met with Rothman, who advised they go back to Point Mugu to prepare and submit a comprehensive 6.2 proposal for Advanced Marine Mammal Research.

They returned to Point Mugu, and over the next several months put together a $200,000 proposal designed to expand the knowledge of marine mammal capabilities following a methodical, progressive, stepwise plan. Armed with this document, they returned to DC and presented their proposal to Sam Rothman. Rothman had invited to the meeting Stan Marcus, the Head of Exploratory Development Research at Naval Sea Systems Command (NAVSEA).

After their presentation, Marcus caught them by surprise. He looked at them and said, "You have it all wrong! You must think bigger and expand this into an ADP so you can really do something" and added, "Of course, you will need an ADO to support your ADP."

Powell recalls what happened next. "Marcus then went to the chalkboard and quickly drew up a broad plan with lines going everywhere." When Marcus had finished, he said, "Now go back to California and resubmit an ADO and ADP within thirty days."

Bill and Woody said "Yes sir", thanked Marcus and Rothman, and left the room as quickly as possible.

"What's an ADP?"

As soon as they were out of earshot in the hall, they looked at each and said "What's an ADP?" Neither of them had ever heard of an ADO or ADP, much less had the slightest idea how to write one.

They soon learned that an ADP stood for "Advanced Development Plan" and an ADO was an "Advanced Development Objective". This was not much help, though, since writing them was beyond their knowledge and skill, and certainly not possible in only thirty days. They were definitely in need of help, and soon.

Once back in California, Bill went directly to see Bill McLean, NOTS Director at China Lake, for advice. McLean told Powell to contact Doug Wilcox, the Technical Director at the Pasadena Lab, because his staff wrote ADPs and ADOs "all the time". So Powell went to Pasadena and met with Wilcox. He asked if Wilcox could assign some of his staff to assist him in writing an ADP and ADO. Wilcox said, simply, "no." He did offer to arrange for Bill to meet with several of his staff that day. But that was another dead end. In this meeting Powell quickly learned they didn't know how to write these documents either!

Meanwhile, back in Point Mugu, Woody also came up empty-handed, discovering that there was no one there who could help write an ADP/ADO.

Bill was becoming concerned. But he persisted in visiting other program managers at China Lake.

At some point, one manager suggested he hire a contractor. Bill checked, and learned that China Lake actually had a contract with two men, Bob Blanchard and Ron Schneider (founders of Integrated Sciences) who wrote ADPs and ADOs.

Powell promptly used McLean's funds to contract them. The Marine Mammal Program's ADP and ADO were completed and submitted to Rothman and Marcus on time, in the spring of 1967. Powell, Woody and other Point Mugu scientists returned to their research and waited to hear back about the proposal.

But the waiting period would not be uneventful.

6

Hangar 102:
Choosing the Site, and the Leadership,
of NUC Hawaii Lab
(1967)

W HILE THE SCIENTISTS AT POINT MUGU BIOSCIENCE
Facility waited to hear from their ONR sponsors regarding their ADP/
ADO submissions, Bill McLean was pursuing his long-held belief that
the Navy needed a place to research new surface vessels, submersibles, and
marine mammals in warm waters. Hawaii was on his radar.

In July 1967, there was a major reorganization of the Navy's Research and
Development Laboratories on the West Coast. McLean would leave NOTS
China Lake and become the Technical Director of the Naval Undersea
Warfare Center (NUWC) temporarily, in Pasadena. Later in February 1969,
the NUWC Headquarters would be moved to San Diego.[1] McLean knew
that the success of this new laboratory structure would require a number
of highly experienced personnel to move to San Diego from their present
labs. McLean also needed a new laboratory to be established somewhere in
Hawaii, which would also require personnel to relocate.

McLean had visited Hawaii several times in the 1960s, and met and befriended Taylor Andrew Prior (known as TAP), the driving force behind the
development of Sea Life Park and the Oceanic Institute in Waimanalo. TAP
was very supportive of the idea of a Navy R&D Laboratory in Hawaii and
promised McLean he would help in any way.

McLean envisioned the Hawaii Lab as small, with an Ocean Engineering
Division, headed by Don Moore from NOTS, and a Marine Mammal

Division, plus a contingent of engineers, scientists, trainers and support personnel.

Don Moore had recommended Richard Boyd, also of NOTS, to head the Marine Mammal Division. Don had observed Boyd's good management skills, and McLean agreed to offer him the job. Unfortunately, Boyd told McLean he thought his career opportunities would be better on the mainland than in Hawaii.

McLean was back to hunting for the right person to head the Marine Mammal Division at the new Hawaii Lab.

The Making of an MMP Manager

Meanwhile, Dan Hightower, a GS-13 engineer, had worked at NOTS for several years primarily conducting rocket propellant and ignition research. He had learned of the new leading-edge submersible vehicle development underway at China Lake supported by McLean. Dan had a chance encounter with McLean and expressed his interest in such ocean engineering projects. They discussed the difficulties and limitation imposed on these projects pursued from a desert location like China Lake and how a Hawaii lab could solve these problems.

McLean had heard good things about Dan's research and his management skills, so he interviewed him in June for the Marine Mammal Program position. McLean told Dan to put together his best resume and go to Point Mugu and interview with Bill Powell, Woody, Sam Ridgway, Bill Evans, and Scott Johnson. They would need to accept him as the Division Head for the Marine Mammal Program (MMP).

Bill Powell was currently serving as "manager" of the Mugu Bioscience Facility with Woody's able assistance. However, neither of them, and none of the other researchers currently there, wanted this new position. His interviews went very well and Powell reported to McLean that Dan would be just fine as their Division Head.

It certainly wasn't a hard sell to Dan on relocating. He and his family had vacationed in Hawaii several times and thought it was an ideal place to live.

With his background in ordnance, he had considering applying for a job in Safety and Quality Assurance at the Lua Lua Lei Ordnance Storage Facility on Oahu. Instead, he would oversee the new Marine Mammal Program.

In Search of a Hawaii Home

In the summer of 1967, McLean had sent Don, Powell, and Woody to survey the Hawaiian Islands and to select the best site for the new NUC Hawaii Lab. They searched the islands for several weeks.

Kaneohe Marine Corps Air Station (KMCAS) was on Kaneohe Bay with clear, warm water and only a short boat ride to very deep water. Due to the deployment of Marines to Vietnam, the base was under-utilized, and had several empty facilities, including one known as Hangar 102. This location seemed ideal.

They returned to China Lake and made their unanimous recommendation to Bill McLean. Soon Marty Conboy and Don McSheehy flew to Hawaii from the Point Mugu Bioscience Facility. Their mission was to conduct dive surveys around KMCAS and select the best site to house and train dolphins, sea lions and even small whales.

Their first choice would have been a large cove on the northern side of the base near the entrance to Kaneohe Bay (later named Sag Harbor). However, this area was already occupied by Pacific Missile Range Facility (PMRF), Hawaii, so the shoreline next to Hangar 102 was their second choice.

Fortunately, a few years later PMRF moved their headquarters from Sag Harbor to Kawai. The property vacated by PMRF provided ideal office space, laboratories, workshops, waterfront facilities and all the necessary infra-structure for the mammal program and emerging ocean engineering research. After this move, only the California sea lions involved in a project called Quick Find remained at Hangar 102 pier.

Hang Up on Hangar 102?

Now, all that remained was to complete the proper paperwork and physically relocate the personnel and animals. McLean told Powell he still had to establish a host-tenant agreement between NOTS and KMCAS. Powell began this by going to the "green eyeshade" guys in the NOTS accounting department. One of the principals involved in writing the agreement was Hal Turner. He had been selected to be the Head Administrator for the new Hawaii Lab.

An agreement was drafted in short order. Powell then flew to Hawaii and presented it to the commanding officer at KMCAS, Col. Arthur Moran. After several modifications by his accounting department, Col. Moran signed the agreement. Powell returned to NOTS with the agreement, which allowed NUC Hawaii to use 50 percent of Hangar 102 as their main facility.

McLean quickly signed the agreement, making it a done deal, or so they thought.

7

"The Hawaii Lab Is Now Open": Building the Hawaii Laboratory from the Bottom Up (Fall 1967)

I N OCTOBER 1967, BILL POWELL, DAN HIGHTOWER, CLARK Bowers, and Hal Turner were about to board an American Airlines flight from LAX to Hawaii. They were embarking on their initial trip to start a laboratory that would develop a SECRET and controversial US Navy program.

As they walked towards the loading ramp to board their flight, an announcement came over the public address system. *"Bill Powell, please go to the nearest courtesy phone… Bill Powell, please go to the nearest courtesy phone."*

They looked at each other. Who would be calling only minutes before takeoff? Bill found a phone at the top of the ramp. Bill McLean was on the line and what he had to say would shock them all.

McLean told Powell that he was worried about the politics of having selected Dan Hightower as head of the Marine Mammal Program (MMP). He now wanted to reconsider his choice because Dan had absolutely no experience with marine mammals, a fact that would be unacceptable to the all-important ONR sponsors.

As the minutes ticked away, McLean went on to list more reasons that made it essential that the position go to Bill. Bill immediately said "No! I don't want the job."

Bill continued to argue against the appointment until airline attendants interrupted and insisted he board immediately or miss his flight. Having lost the argument, Bill told McLean he would take the position but "only if Dan is assigned to work me". McLean said "Okay", and Bill ran down the ramp and took his seat next to Dan.

Noting a bit of stress on Bill's face, Dan asked, "Who was the call from?"

It wasn't easy, but Bill told Dan that he no longer had the job he thought he was traveling to Hawaii to pursue. Then he explained why.

To his credit, Dan responded positively, saying he had no problems with McLean's decision. He pledged his support to Powell and to help in any way possible to make this new and exciting venture succeed.

Dan also promised to be responsible for all hardware engineering needed by the MMP. It looked like now they could move ahead in their efforts to open the new NUC Hawaii Laboratory.

Dirt, Dust, and Empty Oil Drums

The rest of the flight to Hawaii was pleasant and uneventful. Arriving on the island of Oahu, they walked through the little grass huts that served as arrival and departure gates, and immediately knew they were beginning an exciting adventure.

These newly arrived *malahini* Navy lab professionals were soon in sensory overload from the fragrant plumeria leis placed around their necks, sight of palm trees swaying in the gentle trade winds and hula dancers moving gracefully to the rhythmic Polynesian music. After a thirty-minute ride in a rental car from the Honolulu airport to the leeward side of the island, they reached Kailua. After checking in to the Pali Palms Motel near the KMCAS main gate, they went to supper at Florence's Restaurant in Kailua.

They would come to hope that their first evening in Hawaii was not a harbinger of difficulties to come. Celebrating with a few Mai Tai, three of the foursome watched with concern as Hal Turner began to have a serious reaction to the alcohol. Unknown to them, Hal was suffering from severe Type 1 diabetes. At some point in the evening, Hal got into a serious argument with some of the local patrons. The evening ended with Hal narrowly averting a full-blown fist fight.

The next day after breakfast, Hal was back to normal, and they all went to inspect Hangar 102. Here they would have another shock.

Hangar 102 was the vacant building that the base C.O. had agreed, in the host -tenant agreement, could be used for the "new" NUC Hawaii Lab. Bill, Dan, Clark, and Hal entered the hangar and saw nothing but dirt, dust, broken furniture and empty oil drums. They looked at each other, as if to say, *What have we gotten the Navy into?*

An Illegal Phone Line

As they walked around, Dan saw a pile of rotary telephones inside an old oil barrel. He pulled out one that appeared to be intact. Dan, a rocket scientist, took this phone to an electrical panel box on the wall. Inside this box he found several dangling telephone wires. Dan hooked up a red and a green wire to the phone. He then held the phone to his ear and listened for a dial tone. To his surprise they now had a working phone, although they did not know its number and could only call out. (Note: *They used this phone for several weeks. Later when a phone company serviceman came to hook up their new phones, he saw the old phone and asked, "Who did this?" Dan confessed it was him. The phone guy seemed quite upset, and wrote down his name.*)

Bill dialed McLean's phone number from memory. Of course McLean could not see the hangar's condition and didn't have any idea how much work was needed before his "new" Hawaii Lab could be functional. But when McLean answered, Bill said, *"Dr. McLean, the NUC Hawaii Lab is now open."*

"Fish People"

The next day Bill went to see Col. Arthur Moran, the commanding officer, to check on some of the host-tenant agreement details. In another surprise, Col. Moran said that Bill and his "fish people" would have to "slow down a bit". There would be a delay in their moving into Hangar 102, but he didn't say why. Bill politely expressed concern about the delay.

Moran was quick to inform Bill that he got his orders from senior military officers and not civilian scientists. He said he would not change his position on this issue *"unless so ordered by higher military authority"*.

Bill wisely said "Yes sir", and left.

Not sure what to do, he called McLean and told him about his new problem. McLean said, "Don't worry, Sam Rothman at NAVMAT is a friend of the director of Marine Corps Research and may be able to help."

Bill learned later that McLean called Rothman, who called his Marine Corps friend and explained the situation. His friend responded immediately by drafting a telegram for the Commandant of the Marine Corps to sign and send to Lt. General "Brute" Krulack, the Commander of Fleet Marine Force, Pacific (FMFPAC). The telegram was sent with copy to Col. Arthur Moran.

A few days later, Bill was summoned to meet with Col. Moran, who graciously offered to assist with anything he or his people needed. From that day on, Col. Moran and the Marines at KMCAS were extremely helpful in all respects and their relationship thrived. (Note: *Powell later learned that Col. Moran wanted to use Hangar 102 for a retirement ceremony on 1 June, 1968, for Lt. General Krulack. Bill and the lab's personnel accommodated this by partitioning off a large section of the hangar for Krulack's ceremony.*)

After McLean selected Bill Powell to head the Marine Mammal Program at new the Hawaii Lab, he and Dan began working more closely. The ADO/ADP proposals that Bill and Woody had written with contractors (Schneider and Blanchard) were for an Advanced Marine Biological Systems (AMBS) program, also referred to as the Marine Mammal Program (MMP).

Dan recalls sometime in the fall of 1967, he and Bill were requested to fly to DC and explain project details and justify the budget items of their ADP for the MMP. The sponsors from the 3 Navy agencies (OPNAV, NAVSEA, NAVMAT), Stone, Rothman and Marcus were all in attendance. They grilled Powell for hours as he stood before them answering question after question. He frequently used the chalkboard to explain and defend their proposal. Dan sat watching helplessly and felt the tension in the room. Bill was repeatedly pressured to answer questions that were almost impossible to answer at this early stage of the program. Bill was soon sweating profusely and his shirt developed large damp circles under his armpits. The questioning was relentless. Dan, who was there to help with the engineering issues, became increasingly uncomfortable. Finally the questioning ended and the satisfied sponsors thanked Bill and wished them both a nice flight home. Bill and Dan said thanks, walked into the hallway and headed to get a ride to the airport. Once into the hallway, Bill looked at Dan and said "that almost killed me. I never want to do that again."

8

The "Secret Fish People": Early Days of the NUC Hawaii Lab (Late 1967-Early 1968)

N OW NUC HAWAII STARTED TO COLLECT ITS "SECRET fish people". Dan Hightower and his wife Polly, and son, moved to Hawaii the day after Thanksgiving 1967. Bill Powell and his wife, Dolores, and three children arrived the day before Christmas. Clark Bowers and his wife, Zoe, got there a week later, in early January 1968. Now the lab had a complement of three — a project head, an engineer, and a trainer — and half of an empty plane hangar in dire need of major renovations.

Dan Hightower (left) and Bill Powell. Powell and his family arrived in 1967 to start the NUC Hawaii Laboratory. *(Courtesy of Dolores Powell, 1967.)*

In the previous summer, Bill McLean had asked Dan Hightower, as his newly appointed head of the future marine mammal program at the Hawaii Lab, to write a proposal to develop improved tools for Navy divers there. McLean funded Dan's proposal at $37,000, which provided Dan with the funds and a reason to move to Hawaii. Likewise, Clark and Bill were funded at $37,000 for a study to try training wild dolphins in Hawaii.

In January 1968, after getting their families settled into their new environment, Clark and Bill began looking for a seaworthy boat to travel from Oahu to the big island for their study. After a week of searching, they purchased a 25-foot Luhrs.

Also in January, Don McSheehy and his family moved from Point Mugu to Hawaii. Don had been the Director of Animal Training at the Aquatarium in St. Petersburg, Florida. Sam Ridgway had hired him as a civil servant in March 1967 to work at the Point Mugu Bioscience Facility.

After moving to Hawaii, Clark initially was the head trainer, and Don his only trainer. Together they would provide all the husbandry and training for the soon-to-arrive dolphins from Point Mugu and the Florida Keys.

January was a very busy time. Personnel from both NOTS and Point Mugu were making multiple trips from the States to KMCAS and back. Mo Wintermantel, a master at constructing floating pens, had built enough modular components at the Point Mugu Facility to build six floating pens. These components were flown on Navy C-130's to KMCAS and assembled in stages. After the pens were moored off the base shoreline adjacent to Hangar 102 in the Kaneohe Bay, crews delivered two of the defender dolphins: John and Tinker and others from Point Mugu. The other 3 defender dolphins would be captured off Marathon Key later that March and April and transported to the Hawaii Lab.

No one knew it at that point, but in less than a month, the SECRET Marine Mammal Program would be fully funded and ordered by their sponsors to produce results in a shorter period than they thought possible.

II

THE ADVANCE MARINE BIOLOGICAL SYSTEMS BEGIN

(1968-1969)

9

A Million Dollar Call:
Funds for the Advanced Marine
Biological Systems
(8 February 1968)

O N 8 FEBRUARY 1968, BILL POWELL AND CLARK BOWERS
were sitting around a small office table in Hangar 102 planning the details
for their study to attempt training wild dolphins. They heard the phone
ring (the one Dan had unofficially wired). It was Bob Stone of OPNAV calling for Bill. This would be the most important phone call Bill would receive
in the history of the Navy's Swimmer Defense System and Navy Marine
Mammal research.

Bill answered and Bob Stone said, "Congratulations, Bill, your Advanced
Marine Biological Systems Program has been funded for $1.068 million."

This was absolutely great news. The SECRET project was named
STROMAC, an acronym of its sponsors: ST from Bob Stone of OPNAV;
RO from Sam Rothman of NAVMAT; MA from Stan Marcus of NAVSEA;
and C from Jack Collins, Stone's assistant.

The original name suggested by Marcus was MASTRO. But Bob Stone
demanded it be STROMAC since Stone was from OPNAV, the senior
funding agency.

Bill knew exactly what the original research plan required, but he still
asked Stone, "Where do you want us to begin?" Without hesitation, Stone
emphatically said, "Go build a dolphin system to detect and locate swimmers
— and nothing more!"

Stone insisted that they were not to even consider taking on the task of swimmer nullification. He was emphatic that "the dolphin was not to contact the swimmer". (Note: Later this project was unfortunately given the moniker Swimmer Nullification System (SNS), which was entirely incorrect.)

After all the effort Bill, Woody and the Point Mugu researchers had expended, they finally had a mandate from ONR and plenty of money to fund the new Marine Mammal Program. In fact, they had too much money and too little time in which to spend it.

All the project funds ($1.068 million) had to be used in six months (by 31 July 1968). This was the end of the federal government's fiscal year and no funds could be carried over into the next fiscal year.

Bill and Dan Hightower's first action was to go immediately to the Navy's Public Works Department at Pearl Harbor, Hawaii, and set up a construction contract. In short order, they negotiated a $50,000 contract with Public Works to build four more pens and a pier on the shoreline in front of Hangar 102.

Workdays were long and demanding. They hired a wide variety of contractors, such as swimmers, trainers, office and construction personnel, etc., and prepared Hangar 102 for the arrival of administrators, engineers, supply, administrative support, and so on, from various Naval Research laboratories in China Lake, Pasadena, Point Mugu, and San Diego.

Each time a new employee arrived with his family, Bill held a party to celebrate their arrival. This created an informal setting for all families to get to know each other. Dan insists that Bill's plan to hold these parties was "absolutely brilliant". It quickly built strong bonds between co-workers and fostered a very special "esprit de corps" throughout this small yet growing new Navy laboratory.

They would be the ones who trained, designed, engineered, fabricated and supported the development of the Navy's first marine mammal swimmer defense system.

Training the Defender Dolphins (February-May 1968)

Bill Powell, Clark Bowers, and Don McSheehy immediately began designing a chain of behaviors for dolphins that would detect and locate a swimmer — without nullifying or touching the swimmer. They came up with several methods, and pilot-tested some, but none actually located the swimmer. Only one idea had any promise.

Ron Schneider, the contractor who wrote the ADP, suggested they mount a series of response paddles, 360 degrees around the inside of a floating pen. The dolphin would search 360 degrees, and if he detected a swimmer he would push the paddle that was in the direction of the swimmer.

This idea was later modified; the search was changed to only 180 degrees and thus reduced the number of response paddles. This was because the swimmer would generally be approaching from the 180 degrees away from the SVS, and not the 180 degrees behind the SVS. (Note: *We later learned in Vietnam, they would report swimmers anywhere in their area. It soon became obvious that neither of these methods actually located the swimmer. It only provided, at best, the direction or bearing to the swimmer and nothing about the distance to the swimmer. Intense discussions continued between engineers, researchers and trainers. In the end, they concluded that the dolphin had to leave the SVS and swim out and mark the swimmer.*)

Having reached a consensus opinion, and already lost training time, Bill and Clark caught the next flight to Washington, D.C. to convince Bob Stone to change his criteria. Bill went to great length to spell out why it was impossible to know where the swimmer was, without having the dolphin touch or mark the swimmer. Bill argued that since the dolphin can't tell us where the swimmer is, the dolphin has to swim out of the pen and show us.

To Locate and Mark, Only

Stone resisted. He was rightfully concerned that if members of Congress or the public ever thought that the Navy was training dolphins "to kill swimmers", the project would be cancelled. But their arguments made sense. Stone finally acquiesced. "Okay! But don't dare do anything more than mark the swimmer." He added, "The dolphin is *only* to detect and locate *nothing more!*"

Relieved, Bill and Clark returned to Hawaii now confident that they could train a dolphin to detect and "locate/mark" a swimmer. They would also need to capture more dolphins and hire more trainers and swimmers to meet project goals. They needed to have a swimmer detection system ready by May 1969, for a Technical Evaluation of the system in Key West.

The five dolphins flown in from Point Mugu already had some advanced training and were the first to be trained to search and detect swimmers. Each morning the trainers (Don or Clark) took a boat out to two separate dolphin pens anchored in the bay. Each took a bag lunch, a small ice chest with beverages, a small stool, a pinger and a bucket of iced fish. Each sat on the stool along the walkway of the pen and trained a dolphin. Each pen had three response paddles mounted inside the pen. The "Station" paddle was directly in front of the trainer. The two "Response" paddles were separated by two feet and 180 degrees at the opposite side of the pen.

Training was individualized for each dolphin, depending on their personality, time in captivity, prior training history, and so on. Newly captured dolphins had to first be trained to reliably perform a set of basic behaviors before they could be trained more advanced (complex) behaviors. These behaviors must be carefully conditioned, shaped, maintained and chained together to become a continuous series of actions.

DOLPHIN TRAINING 101 AND 102

Basic Dolphin Training

Feeding. Wild dolphins don't eat dead fish, and for good reasons. So immediately after capture, the trainer introduces dead fish while feeding the dolphin live fish. It sometimes takes a while to convert them to eat only dead fish. The time will vary depending on degree of hunger, feeding behavior of adapted pen mates (e.g., competition for the food) and use of vitamin supplements (B^{12}). Experienced trainers have several approaches and methods of overcoming blocks/impasses in training any behavior. The Navy trainers first learned by watching the civilian trainers and asking questions, listening and understanding their answers. Later we would take our training problems to them and learn how they handled a particular situation.

Stationing. An extremely important basic behavior is added after eating dead fish has become routine. The trainer presents a signal/stimulus (e.g., placing a hand in the water or slapping a fish on the surface) that the dolphin can feel, see or hear. When the dolphin comes to this stimulus. it is rewarded. This leads to using a pinger (of a given frequency) as the stimulus because it will become a "recall signal" that brings the dolphin to the trainer under all conditions.

Because of its importance, our dolphins were always rewarded for returning to a recall pinger and *touching it.* Touching the pinger completes the behavior chain and allows the trainer to know the dolphin has returned even in the dark. Merely returning to the vicinity of the recall is not considered sufficient to receive a fish. The requirement to touch the pinger is critical to training the next basic behavior.

Gate Training. Dolphins do not encounter gates in the wild (nor many nets). For some reason, dolphins will not swim through constricted openings (e.g., between pilings or gates in a pen) unless trained to do so. All open-ocean control dolphins must be trained to go in and out holding pens and the netted enclosure of an SVS. After recall training becomes a reliable behavior, it is a valuable tool used in gate training. There are several ways to accomplish gate training. Below is but one.

The trainer opens the dolphin's gate and then places the recall pinger, immediately in front of the opening outside the pen. If the dolphin comes and touches the pinger he gets a reward (fish). After a short wait, the trainer repeats this but now the pinger is very near the gate opening. If the dolphin touches the pinger again, he gets a reward.

The trainer repeats this sequence and requires the dolphin to go progressively farther into the opening. The dolphin eventually (not always) becomes more comfortable with this foreign structure. Good trainers know just when this has occurred and then put the pinger clearly inside the pen. This is the biggest step in gate training and requires an "aha" moment for the dolphin. Now the dolphin must decide if it's worth leaving the pen to touch the pinger to get a reward. Once a dolphin will go in and out to touch the pinger, this is only the beginning because this behavior must be maintained and strengthened for a while before it becomes a non-issue.

Advanced Training

At the start of the STROMAC dolphin training, the dolphins had to be taught to push one paddle for no swimmer present and the other paddle for swimmer present. This may seem like a simple task, but it's not.

Since we can't talk to dolphins and explain what we want them to do, we must pair stimuli (tones, swimmers, etc.) with rewards for correct behavior responses (paddle push, echolocation search, respond to swimmer present, or absent, etc.). The dolphin was first trained to push the "station" paddle every time he heard a tone of a specific frequency from a hydrophone behind a paddle in front of the trainer.

At a predetermined time interval, the trainer signaled the dolphin to push the station paddle, then turn to the right and make a 180-degree search for a swimmer. After completing the search, the dolphin pushed either the positive (swimmer present) or negative (no swimmer) paddle at the opposite end from the station paddle.

Swimmers waited on surfboards anchored, in a large arc at variable distances, and bearings from the left side of the pen. Before signaling the dolphin to station and search, the trainer signaled one of the swimmers to slip off his surfboard and tread water. Using these operant conditioning techniques, the trainers established, shaped and over time improved and maintained the dolphin's search patterns and marking behaviors. After the dolphins acquired the proper search behavior, their time on station was extended and food reward size reduced to last longer.

Sag Harbor offices, dolphin pens, and whale enclosure. *(U.S. Navy. Used by permission.)*

When a dolphin responded with a positive, indicating a swimmer present, it was re-interrogated to confirm its original positive. This required a second search to reduce the number of false positives. After a confirmed positive the trainer quickly took a custom-made nosecup to the edge of the pen and placed it on the dolphin's rostrum and opened the pen gate. The Hawaii Lab engineers designed the nosecup based on a prototype from the Point Mugu facility.

The dolphin swam quickly out towards the swimmer (breaking the surface only to breathe) and pushed the nosecup against the back or side of the swimmer. This released a buoyant, waterproof strobe light that marked the swimmer in day or night.

The swimmer signaled the trainer indicating the location and quality of the dolphin's contact. This allowed the trainer to reward or withhold, depending on the final response in this complex chain of behaviors.

The reason the dolphins were required to contact the swimmer in the back quadrant of his body was to avoid retaliation from an enemy swimmer. The dolphin was also trained to return immediately to its trainer and pen. If the dolphin ever lingered around the swimmer, it was not rewarded.

This phase of the training was not difficult because the sequence was initially trained, close to the pen, so the trainer could shape and strengthen the entire sequence of behaviors. The last stage was to gradually move the swimmer farther and farther out at random bearings. This required many surfboards and swimmers.

Kaneohe Bay was known for having a season when hammerhead sharks were present in numbers. This motivated some swimmers to find alternative employment, or to pay others swimmers to take their place during this season.

10

Secret Duty:
Becoming the Navy's First
Marine Mammal Officer
(January-May 1969)

FTER COMPLETING NINE MONTHS OF SEA DUTY ON the aircraft carrier Shangri-la (CVA-38), I was assigned shore duty at EOD Group Atlantic (EODGRULANT), at Fort Story, Virginia in December, 1968. I was given a desk job in the Operations Department, headed by CDR Tom Kelly. Our task was to provide EOD teams for a variety of missions involving ordnance (e.g., ships, shore facilities, ordnance accidents, and special projects).

This was a welcomed change after sea duty. On shore duty, life was more normal without the taste of JP-5 in the "bug juice," water, and coffee. I now worked eight-hour days without night duty on the flight deck or restricted to a closed space (without air-conditioning) for hours during General Quarters (GQ) drills. However, after only a few months of seeing guys go off to interesting places to perform real EOD jobs, I was ready for a Temporary Additional Duty (TAD) assignment. I made a point to be one of the first to read incoming messages in hopes of finding an interesting TAD job.

To my surprise, in late January 1969, the Technical Evaluation Detachment (TEVDET) Key West sent a message requesting EOD divers to assist with a high priority project. Apparently, the project had fallen behind schedule because their EOD divers were running out of bottom time. If they had two more divers, the project could be completed in four weeks. A month of diving in Key West in the middle of winter sounded just great to me.

I hurried to see the Ops Officer because many other officers would certainly volunteer for this job. Luckily, I found CDR Kelly alone in his office and handed him the message. He carefully read it and then asked if I wanted this TAD. I said, "Yes," and gave him my best pitch. I said I was a Floridian with broad aquatic experiences. I snorkeled and dove in the Keys and worked on my department's research vessel while majoring in Biology at the University of Florida. He looked up and said "I'll let you know tomorrow."

The next day, I was called to CDR Kelly's office along with Boatswain mate 1st class Bobby Joe Pippin, the hardest working EOD diver partner I ever had. CDR Kelley sent us to the Personnel Department to pick up our TAD orders to TEVDET, Key West for four weeks. This was later extended an additional four weeks, due to weather delays. We were there from 27 January to 29 March 1969.

Off to Key West

We reported to TEVDET on 27 January and went directly to the EOD Detachment to store our dive gear and meet the O-in-C, LDO Lt. Tew. Bobby Joe was a burly, proud sailor and usually wore a small silver earring in his left ear. Even though it was not officially allowed, it looked just perfect on him. Lt. Tew was a by-the-book, Bible-thumping, conservative Southern Baptist who gave Bobby Joe the evil eye every time he saw him.

After a few days Tew insisted I tell Bobby Joe not to wear his earring on base. I picked a time and place to politely ask Bobby Joe to take his earring off before coming on base, and especially to never wear it around Lt. Tew. His first response was to give me a brief history of the tradition of earrings and beards in the American and other navies of the world. I looked up at this six-foot-two Popeye-like sailor and simply said, "Bobby Joe, I don't have a problem with your earring, but I'm not the Officer-in-Charge here."

He nodded and reluctantly said "Okay, boss."

Before returning to EODGRULANT, Bobby Joe had logged more dives, worked more days, excavated more bombs, and had more bottom time than Lt. Tew and all his men combined. Bobby Joe (without his earring) volunteered to help Lt. Tew's EOD team successfully pass a "Broken Arrow" drill, their annual Nuclear Technical Proficiency Inspection (NTPI). A few days later, he helped Tew's team disarm an F-4B Phantom that had crashed at the nearby Boca Chica, Naval Air Station.

Testing for 'Pocket Money'

The first workday Bobby Joe and I were briefed on the TEVDET project. We learned they were testing MK-36 Destructors (DSTs) for the future mining of Haiphong Harbor (North Vietnam's largest port). Later I learned that in 1967 the "Nimrod Study" had taken the MK-82 low drag bomb plus a MK-75 kit and developed the MK-36 DST, which then could be used as a land or bottom mine. The mining of Haiphong Harbor (code name "Operation Pocket Money") could not begin until the MK-36 DST had been properly tested under bottom conditions similar to Haiphong Harbor. TEVDET Key West was conducting these tests during Jan-March of 1969.

Slightly more than three years later, on 9 May 1972, President Nixon launched Operation Pocket Money with Navy A-6s and A-7s from the aircraft carrier Coral Sea, by dropping 36 mines (such as Mk-52, MK-53 and MK-54s) in the inner and outer channel of Haiphong Harbor. Over the next eight months, the Navy re-seeded the harbor, dropping 108 more mines plus 11,000 MK-36 DSTs. The goal was to deter ships from re-supplying the North Vietnam Army (NVA) and Viet Cong (VC) in the South, and thus help protect U.S. and Vietnamese troops during the U.S. withdrawal.

The TEVDET project tested only inert MK-36 DSTs with detonators set at different magnetic sensitivities. The bombs now "mines", were configured with "Snake Eye" fin assemblies which retarded drop speed and impact. They were test-dropped from low flying F-4 Phantom jets into 20 to 35 feet of water. The test area was southwest of Key West just off Woman, Man and Ballast Keys. To help locate the dropped bombs, fluorescent green dye was painted on the bombs' noses. Additionally, upon impact. a 25-foot length of quarter-inch yellow polyethylene line deployed from the tail fin assembly. The F-4s made low level runs and usually dropped four bombs while we observed the impacts from a nearby Boston Whaler. We drove to the impact sites and jumped in the water and located the bomb or bottom entry point and marked it with a buoy. Some bombs didn't penetrate the bottom ("proud") others penetrated and then traveled some distance below the surface ("buried").

Using our buoy markers, TEVDET vessels later made passes over the "mines" to activate the fuse mechanisms by emitting known magnetic signals. We recovered these "mines" and returned them to TEVDET where the fuses were examined for functioning. The few "proud" mines were easily recovered by connecting them to a cable and hoisting them aboard the barge. However, most mines were buried. These required much more time and effort. For these we used a P-500 (500 gal/min) washout hose ("fire hose") and an airlift (underwater "vacuum cleaner"). With the airlift and washout hose, we would excavate up to fifteen feet along a bomb's path. I had never heard of an airlift before, but I thoroughly enjoyed this very interesting recovery work.

Gone Fishing

We always dove in pairs for an hour or an hour and a half at a time, so even with six divers, we often used up our bottom time by 1300-1400. On days with strong southern or easterly winds, diving operations were canceled. On these days we speared fish, and caught lobsters and stone crabs in protected areas off Key West. Having a good number of cancelled or short dive days, my wife, Sharon left Virginia and joined me. She escaped one of the coldest winters ever recorded for Virginia Beach.

Together we had many successful days spear fishing and collecting delicious crustaceans. We stored quite a trove of seafood before I was recalled to EODGRULANT, so that other divers could gain diving experiences from this project.

Back at EODGRULANT

Soon after returning to EODGRULANT, I was summoned to see my Commanding Officer, CAPT Oliver, who wanted to be briefed on the TEVDET project. This meeting would definitely be the *most critical event in my Navy career and life.*

During the meeting I described in detail what we had done. At some point CAPT Oliver asked about our encounters with dangerous marine life, such as sharks, barracuda, and moray eels. I said I had not seen any sharks but occasionally did see barracudas. He asked if the barracuda were a problem. I told him they rarely attack divers because they are smarter and more discriminating than sharks. I offered to loan him a book I had on the topic[1] and dropped it off the next day.

Within a week I was told CAPT Oliver wanted to see me again. I thought maybe he wanted to return my book or talk more about barracuda. To my surprise, he said he had been requested to recommend an EOD Officer with a Biology degree to work with a SECRET project in Hawaii. He said that if I wanted this job, I would have to pass an interview and extend my active duty commitment two years.

He let me call my wife, Sharon. After a short conversation with her, I returned and told him I wanted this assignment. He wasted no time in getting me travel orders to the Pentagon, and the next day I drove there for an interview.

I had visited Washington, DC several times but had never been inside the Pentagon. I parked in the south lot and followed the directions I had been given, up to the point where I got lost and asked for assistance. This happened several times as I walked through the seemingly endless concentric rings of windowless wide halls. The directions led me deeper and deeper into the core of this huge building.

Finally I arrived at a door with the correct number. Fortunately it had a speaker phone outside. I pushed the button and announced myself and said I was here to see Dr. Collins. Someone opened the door and said "Follow me."

The man led me through a series of thick, heavy, steel doors that reminded me of safes. He had to punch a series of buttons before we could enter. Finally we arrived at an unpretentious office area, where my escort introduced me to Dr. Jack Collins.

He was a studious-looking gentleman with thinning gray hair. He was wearing dark slacks, a long sleeve white shirt and no tie. He shook my hand

and politely offered me a chair. He asked about my interest in biology and why I had chosen to be in EOD. Then he described the new assignment. He paused and asked if I had questions. I had only a few, which he answered.

He then said, "Do you want this job?" I replied, "Yes sir, definitely."

"Okay, you have the job. However, you have to be in Key West in two weeks to join this project," he said.

Since we had just been in Key West for two months, I worked hard to hold back a smile. He went on to say that after a month, with the project in Key West, I would go to San Diego and check in at my new command, the Naval Undersea Research and Development Center (NURDC). Then I would proceed to my final destination, NURDC's Hawaii Laboratory at Kaneohe Marine Corps Air Station.

This was indeed a dream come true.

He summoned his assistant, who helped me complete the paperwork for a one-year extension to my active duty obligation. Again, I had to hold back my emotions, since I had expected a two-year extension. After I finished the paperwork, Dr. Collins asked if I needed anything else.

"Yes sir, I would really like someone to show me how to get out to my car," I said.

He smiled and had his assistant take me to the outer ring of the Pentagon maze. I finally made it outside and found my car in the huge parking lot.

Driving home to Virginia Beach, I was filled with excitement and anticipation. My mind was racing. Wow, we were going back to Key West, on to California and then to Hawaii!

We would have to pack our household goods, ship them to Hawaii, and return to Key West, where we had been only four weeks earlier. One of my first thoughts was, *what are we going to do with all the great seafood we just brought back from Key West?*

YOU CAN'T TAKE IT WITH YOU:
A FAREWELL SEAFOOD FEAST AND A LOADED WHALE
(30 APRIL 1969)

When I returned home from my interview at the Pentagon, Sharon agreed that our biggest problem was not packing our household goods. It was deciding what to do with a year's supply of frozen seafood we had brought back from Key West.

Short on time and options, we decided to have a "farewell, all-you-can-eat seafood party". We invited all the EOD officers at EODGRULANT. We served lobster tails, stone crabs, hog snapper and grouper fillets prepared several ways. Some guys were eating lobster tails like they were cocktail shrimp. Sharon kept cooking in our small kitchen well into the late evening. She fried filets of grouper and snapper that had been dipped in a mixture of 7-Up and pancake batter or flour. Other fillets were coated with French dressing or crushed Cheeze-Its and then baked. She made a crab dip for crackers, and served chucks of stone crab claw meat in bowls to be dipped in drawn butter with Key Lime juice.

Then there was "Flinks' wine". I had made two gallons of the stuff from a recipe our Key West neighbors shared (Welch's Grape Juice, Baker's yeast, and a gallon glass jug sealed with a strong balloon), which we couldn't take with us either. It wasn't as big a hit as the fish, except with one officer who ended up spending the night in our bathtub. The next day he managed to make his way to his car, but was complaining of severe stomach cramps and headaches. (I have never made "Flinks' wine" since.)

The Loaded Whale Fiasco

The talk of the party was a fiasco that would become an EODGRULANT legend. It lives on today in the hearts and minds of all the East Coast EOD officers and men who wear the "Charles County Crab" (the EOD insignia).

It's the tale of the loaded whale. And it wasn't loaded with Flinks' wine.

The day before the party, Ltjg. Les Bivens (who later became the Navy's Third Marine Mammal Officer) was the Command Duty Officer at EODGRULANT when a request came for assistance in disposing of a dead whale that had washed up on Virginia Beach. Bivens recalls that our X.O., CDR Henry Staples, wanted to person-ally coordinate this operation, and hand-picked an EOD team to work with him. The team cut four holes in its side and packed each with a twenty-pound satchel of C-4 (a total of 80 pounds of plas-tic explosives). They also primed the satchels with blasting caps, time fuse and a manual igniter. Following standard operating pro-cedures, they ignited a known length of fuse on the sand and timed its burn. They then cut a length of fuse that would guarantee a safe separation time later when they ignited the time fuses.

The Coast Guard had agreed to assist in this operation by towing the whale offshore so the team could ignite the time fuses and blow up the whale. This way the explosion wouldn't scatter the whale carcass all over the beach area (a problem that was not unknown). The command had contacted a whale expert at the Smithsonian Institute in Washington, D.C. who had assured them that a dead whale "will float".

So with the primed charges properly secured in the whale, a Coast Guard vessel began towing the whale off the beach. The plan was to pull the whale through the surf zone and then out to sea. Once well offshore and clear of any vessels, the EOD team would drive to the whale, yell "fire in the hole", then pull the four igniters. Then they would quickly drive away to the required safe distance and wait for the explosion.

However, to everyone's surprise, just as the whale was outside the surf zone and moving into deeper water, the towline broke ...and the whale immediately sunk below the surface. The Coast Guard and EOD boats searched until darkness forced them to stop for the night. EODGRULANT was now responsible for a whale primed with 80 pounds of plastic explosives, adrift, without lights or markers, in the heavily trafficked waters near the entrance to the Chesapeake Bay, the home to the U.S. Navy's largest active fleet. At this point, the command had only one, but very embarrassing, option. That was to broadcast an emergency, "Notice to Mariners", warning that there was a primed whale adrift somewhere off the Virginia shoreline.

For the next few days (and nights) CDR Staples and other EOD personnel drove jeeps up and down the Virginia coast searching for the whale. A week or so later the whale washed up on a desolate stretch of beach, well south of Virginia Beach. Bivens and I can't be sure, but we are relatively certain that a different EOD team was sent this time to blow it up.

11

Ambush in a Barber Shop:
Surprise First Encounter with Dan Hightower
(7-8 May 1969)

A FEW DAYS AFTER THE SEAFOOD FEAST WAS HELD AT our home in Virginia Beach, Sharon and I headed back to Key West. In route, we spent a few days visiting our families in Ocala, Florida, then continued on to Key West. We arrived on Tuesday, 7 May, and I checked in with my TAD orders at the Naval Ordnance Unit (NOU).

We were very familiar with Key West and knew where to rent an efficiency apartment on the southern end of the island. We had two days before the special military flight, from the Hawaii Laboratory with project equipment and personnel, would land at Boca Chica Naval Air Station (five miles from Key West). I had been told that one of the civilians, Dan Hightower, from this SECRET project, would fly in from Miami, the day before the main group. I was also given the name of his hotel. I decided to go over and introduce myself after he arrived.

In 1969, there was only one flight a day and it was very easy to know when it arrived. Anyone outside could easily see or hear the twin engine commuter coming in for its landing. Earlier that year, I had flown in and out of Key West on the same small commuter plane when I was on TAD working on Project Pocket Money.

The next day I heard the plane arrive and waited about twenty-five minutes to allow Dan to get to his motel. I walked the few short blocks to the motel and went to the front desk and asked if Dan Hightower had checked in. The desk clerk said yes, but that Dan wanted a haircut so he told him there was a barber shop two blocks away on Duval Street.

Without thinking about how it might appear, I walked to the barber shop and paused outside the window to survey the customers. There was only one man in a barber chair and he was wearing a Hawaiian shirt. I went inside, walked up, and said, "You must be Dan Hightower."

Dan was dumbfounded.

His reaction makes complete sense. Consider the following; he was working on a highly classified SECRET project and had flown alone from Hawaii across the Pacific Ocean and the continental United States to Miami. He spent the night there and the next day flew directly to Key West. He had gone straight to his motel and before unpacking, had walked directly to this little barber shop. All this time he had spoken to almost no one. How could this total stranger find him so quickly?

After he acknowledged he was, in fact, Dan Hightower, I introduced myself and sat down on one of the vinyl-covered chromed frame chairs and waited while the Cuban-American barber finished Dan's haircut. Walking back to his motel, I described my previous Navy assignments and my strong desire to become a marine biologist. Dan explained the purpose of the upcoming test and summarized the plans and scheduled events.

This was indeed another critical point in my career, and a meeting that was burned into my memory. I had just met the very first person from the SECRET dolphin project. For the next two years, I worked with Navy scientists, civilian trainers, engineers and military personnel on STROMAC and Project Short Time. Together we developed, tested and deployed the Navy's first operational marine mammal system. This experience permanently altered my life.

12

Deployment to Key West:
Testing the Long-Distance Capability
of the System
(8 May-10 June 1969)

FTER OUR MEETING AT THE BARBER SHOP, DAN
Hightower and I agreed to drive the next day to Boca Chica Naval Air
Station and meet the equipment flight from NUC Hawaii. Here I would
begin learning how all the system equipment was off-loaded and assembled.

This was the first of several times I observed and participated in a C-141
offload. The whole operation was very interesting to watch. The loadmaster
was totally and unequivocally in charge of everything. Nothing on the plane
moved an inch without his approval.

The offloaded equipment was staged in separate areas (boats, trailers and
engines, dolphin related material, and electronic/electrical equipment). The
NUC team had divided into smaller groups and each began assembling their
specialized project equipment. The team building the dolphin pens placed
the netting, barrel floats and pre-cut and numbered wooden walkways, onto a
large flat-bed truck. A crane placed the modified pontoon boat (SVS) on another flatbed truck. This made the boat, with its eight-foot-high cabin, tower
high above the road.

I later learned that Marty Conboy and Bill Steele had visited Key West a
month earlier to conduct a site survey to check out and inspect everything. It's
quite a coincidence that I remembered seeing them talking with Lt. Tew (the
EOD Detachment O-in-C) one day when I was there on TAD recovering
mines for Project Pocket Money. (Marty was unforgettable with his goatee
and floppy hat.) He and Bill had measured the height and width of all gates

and overhead obstructions (power lines, road overpasses, entrance signs, etc.) along the route from the Boca Chica airfield to the quay wall where the pens and SVS would be lowered into the water.

The first and most important task was to take the pen materials to the pier on Truman Annex and assemble them for the dolphins. The animal flight would arrive the next day and the pens had to be ready.

One of the objectives of the technical evaluation was to see how long it would take the dolphins to adapt to a new environment and perform their trained behaviors. This was the first time they had been required to travel this far in stretchers and then immediately perform their swimmer defense behaviors. Previously, trainers had conducted a test by flying several dolphins in a C-130 from KMCAS around the islands for several hours before landing at Hickam Air Force Base. Here they were off-loaded, transported to a Navy facility, and placed in the water to perform searching and marking behaviors. This of course was nothing like the 8,000-mile flight from KMCAS to Key West on the Atlantic Ocean. No one knew for certain how the dolphins would perform.

The next day, the dolphins arrived and were taken directly to Truman Annex where they were placed in pens. After adapting to being in water again they were boat-followed, one at a time, to the prototype SVS which operated in the Key West channel. Having only one SVS, the five dolphins rotated on sentry duty. Most test swims were at night and simulated a sapper attack on a ship, moored to a pier they were guarding.

This was my first contact with the dolphins I would work with for the next two years. This also was my first contact with all the managers, engineers, trainers and supporting members of STROMAC (including Conboy, Bill Powell, Don McSheehy, Clark Bowers, Larry Phillips, Bob Flood, Harry Chalmers, and others).

I was impressed with their dedication and work ethic and their ability to enjoy being together after work was over. We were very fortunate that Bill Steele had recently been the O-in-C of the Key West EOD Det. and become a close friend of a surgeon named Dr. Lance Lester, and his family. Dr. Lester was an avid diver who took us to spear-fishing sites where we did quite well.

Dr. Lance Lester (left) and Bill Steele, with a 200-pound Jewfish in Lester's backyard. Lester was a surgeon and diver who opened his house in Key West to the Hawaii Lab personnel.*(Author's photo, 1969.)*

Scott Henderson, Bill Steele, Milo McManus, with Dr. Lance Lester's daughter, Georgina, celebrating spearing a 150-160-pound Jewfish off Key West. *(Author's Photo, 1969.)*

The fish were cleaned and cooked at his home while we played snooker pool and sipped wine and beers.

Sharon was a great help and performed the chef duties in the Lesters' kitchen. I was the only one who had his wife along on this trip. She and Dr. Lester's daughter, Georgina, were the only females around this very interesting group of special guys. Lester's wife was out of town visiting relatives in Miami.

For four weeks (8 May-10 June) we conducted day and night swims against the dolphins. Those who were off went fishing and skin diving during the day. Each evening, we generally ate late but always had great food, often at Dr. Lester's home. Some nights we went to the Hukilau Restaurant and Lounge opposite Garrison Bight on Roosevelt Boulevard. Here we ate well and listened and laughed as Coffee Butler played piano and sang his original songs, often until the lounge closed.

We never had it so good. To this day, everyone along on this test remembers the wonderful diving, meals, joy, and friendship we experienced that month of our lives.

13

Heading for Hawaii:
Unique Duty for a Young EOD Officer
and His Wife
(15-19 June 1969)

N EARLY JUNE, 1969, THE UNOFFICIAL TECHNICAL
Evaluation of the Swimmer Defense System was completed at Key West.
The program manager, civilian trainers, technicians, engineers and dolphins
all flew back to the laboratory at KMCAS in Hawaii. I would soon join them,
but first I had to check into my new command, the Naval Undersea Research
and Development Center (NURDC) in San Diego.

Sharon and I drove five days across the country, stopping in Panama City,
Florida; Natchez, Mississippi; central Texas; and El Paso. We finally arrived
in San Diego late Wednesday afternoon on 18 June. We had made arrange-
ments to spend the night with my roommate from Navy Officer Candidate
School (OCS), Jim Kellerman, and his wife, Kathy. They lived in an apartment on Nimitz Boulevard in the Point Loma area of San Diego, only a short
distance from NURDC. That night they took us to a great Mexican meal at
the La Piñata restaurant in Old Town. We talked about our experiences after
OCS over more bottles of Corona than I can remember.

The next day after breakfast, I buffed up my black shoes, shined my
belt buckle and put on my Tropical Khaki uniform, pinned on my EOD
Technician badge and single "gedunk" ribbon (National Defense), both properly aligned on my shirt. My Khaki cover was no longer new but still quite
acceptable. I wiped the brim with a moist handkerchief and adjusted the gold
braided strap, making certain all my "eagles were flying". The next step was to

have Sharon help me with a "military tuck" for my shirt. Finally, I aligned my shirt, belt tip, buckle and fly, being careful not to lose my military tuck.

I was now ready to meet my new C.O. I said good-bye to Sharon and carefully eased into the seat of our 1967 Pontiac LeMans, carefully preserving my military shirt tuck.

Unfamiliar with San Diego, I allowed plenty of time for the short drive to NURDC, just in case something went wrong. Jim and Kathy had told me I needed to only make one turn after leaving their apartment, and I had no problem finding NURDC. This was a Navy Research and Development base comprised mainly of civilian researchers, headed by Dr. William (Bill) B. McLean, the Technical Director, and Navy CAPT Charles Bishop. Military personnel (like me) were assigned to the laboratory, primarily to advise the civilian scientists and engineers who designed, developed and tested ordnance and equipment for Navy applications.

I parked just inside the gate and walked to the Military office being careful not to scuff my shoes or pull out my tuck. The Military Office was in an older, single story wooden building with steps leading to the main door that opened directly into a short hall and the reception area. I walked up the steps, removed my cover, went inside, and introduced myself to the two ladies behind desks.

One was Thelma Flowers, Bill McLean's secretary, and the other was the Captain's Secretary, Betty Box (yes, that was her name). I handed Betty my orders and told her I had been assigned to the Hawaii Laboratory but needed to report in here to Captain Bishop. She said that the C.O. was on the phone but should be finished soon, and asked me to please have a seat.

I went over to the couch and sat down. In the process, there was a clearly audible "rrrrrip" sound ... from the seat of my pants. I had just split the threads completely down the middle of my pants!

Oh boy! I was embarrassed beyond words. I was about to meet my new Commanding Officer, and I had gone to great effort to impress him with my "flying eagles", shiny shoes, shiny belt buckle, uniform alignments, and of course that very sharp military tuck Sharon had given me! I couldn't possibly meet the C.O. with the seat of my pants wide open and my under shorts showing.

I looked helplessly over to the two secretaries and in a soft voice said, "Excuse me, but I just ripped my pants and I don't know what to do."

To my great relief, Thelma saved my day. "Don't worry. I keep a sewing kit here in my drawer. You go over to the men's room, take off your pants and pass them out to me. I'll stitch them up."

I was certain she was an angel sent from heaven. I did exactly as she said but soon realized that I was standing half-dressed in the only men's room in the office area. I became self-conscious and prayed that no one would come in and see me wearing only my undershorts, shiny black shoes, khaki shirt with squared away gedunk ribbon and EOD badge. My prayer was answered, and no one came into the restroom. Thelma soon knocked on the door and handed me my pants. I went out to the reception room just in time to be told that I could now go meet CAPT Bishop.

I don't know if he ever learned about my little problem, and what Thelma had done to save a young and very embarrassed Naval Officer. Somehow this young officer later became a Captain and holds great respect and appreciation for all those who helped him in his career. Thelma ranks near the top of that list.

Oh yes, my meeting with CAPT (Charlie) Bishop went very well, even if the military tuck I had worked so hard to preserve was now history. He was quite cordial, easy to speak with, and one of the best Commanding Officers I had in my Navy career. He was an oceanographer and highly qualified to be C.O. of NURDC, soon renamed the Naval Undersea Center (NUC). He retired as NUC's C.O. in September 1972, and became Assistant Director of the Marine Physical Laboratory at Scripps Institution of Oceanography, and at this writing still lives in San Diego.

The rest of the day was relatively uneventful. Sharon and I had been told that a large gas-guzzling car would not be the best vehicle for Hawaii because of high gas prices and the lack of highways. We traded the LeMans in for a new red Volkswagen with automatic/stick shift. The next day we began a three-day drive to Travis Air Force Base, where we dropped off our VW for overseas shipping.

Then we flew to Hickam AFB, Honolulu. Here we were greeted by friends we made during the one month Technical Evaluation in Key West. They presented us with beautiful aromatic plumaria leis and aloha gifts, then drove us to Kailua where we could rent a car. We checked in at the KMCAS BOQ where we stayed a few days before getting temporary lodging off-base. Soon we settled in and began our two-year tour at the NUC Hawaii Lab.

We never dreamed Sharon would acquire a Secret Clearance and be hired as a dolphin trainer for Michael Greenwood's short-lived job as project manager. (See Appendix VI-B) However, that is another story.

14

The Day the Project Died:
Navy SEALs Torpedo the
Dolphin Swimmer Defense System
(December 1969)

THE NEXT FOUR MONTHS WERE PACKED WITH LEARNing about marine mammals.

Our small military detachment of seven EOD Techs (two Officers and five Chiefs) plus a Boatswain Mate and an Ocean Systems Tech Striker, worked alongside NUC's civilian trainers. We learned basic and advanced behavioral conditioning techniques, anatomy of dolphins and sea lions, proper animal husbandry, animal health monitoring and medical care. We knew how to thaw, bucket and insert vitamins in the different types (species) of fish. We maintained charts recording the types and amounts of fish and vitamins each dolphin ate. We were experienced at cleaning and sanitizing fish buckets and all surfaces in the fish house area, to the point we could pass a U.S. Health Department's inspection.

We learned the importance of early detection of behavioral problems and how to apply remedial, corrective, and maintenance training. After working with us for months, the civilian trainers stepped back and only observed us and commented on our performance. During these few months, we had learned an enormous amount about dolphins and specifically about the dolphin we trained regularly. Working in two-man teams we rotated training responsibilities with a civilian and later, only with another military trainer. Most of the time, the alternate trainer became the simulated attacking swimmer and was dropped off in the bay, and swam towards a target in the dolphin's surveillance area.

Most of the military graduated from Boat Driver/Dolphin Handler to become a primary Dolphin Trainer. Though we worked in pairs, one person normally was the primary trainer for one of the five dolphins (Garth, John, Slan, Tinker or Toad). The civilians were primary trainers for only one dolphin (except for Don McSheehy and Clark Bowers, who could train all five dolphins).

During the twelve months before the military arrived in the summer of 1969, Scott Henderson trained Toad, Brooks Robbins trained Tinker, Don trained John, Larry Landis and Mike Schultz trained Garth, and Milo McManus trained Slan. Additionally, there were contract trainers: Ralph Hawn, Chuck Loving, George Peabody, and George Lingle. All but Lingle had left the lab before the military personnel arrived.

Don, Clark, and a few other civilian trainers often met informally at the Pali Palms with military trainers after work. In this relaxed, nonthreatening setting (and with a few Primos), we could discuss dolphin behavioral issues and potential solutions without losing face (a real issue for some older Navy Chiefs).

It was at informal events like this that we learned there were several effective techniques to correct a given behavioral problem. The civilians also confirmed the military trainers' suspicions that each dolphin was unique and learned tasks at different rates, and often had idiosyncrasies. Each dolphin needed to be treated individually, depending on the conditions and circumstances. We learned that if we were not attentive to what we rewarded, we may find ourselves being trained by the dolphin.

The unofficial, Technical Evaluation of the Dolphin Swimmer Defense System (May-June 1969) in Key West was highly successful but used only civilian trainers. It was now time to repeat this test with only military trainers. Learning how to use operant conditioning technology was a challenge for even the handpicked EOD technicians. At that time, I wondered if any other Navy unit had the commitment, patience, and skill set (academics, swimming/diving, boat handling and maintenance, rigging, and ordnance disposal experience) necessary to accomplish this task. Our civilian counterparts had become professional trainers after many years of working with animals at ocean parks.

Our military unit had much to learn about maintaining high levels of performance. A civilian trainer (Milo) was assigned as a technical representative to assist us during the early days of our deployment to Vietnam. Additionally, we were extremely fortunate to have TD-1 Bill Scronce (Navy Training Deviceman, First Class) join our detachment in December 1971. Scronce had years of animal training experience at Point Mugu and professional instructions from experts like Kent Burgess, and Drs. Keller and Marian Breland at Animal Behavior Enterprises (ABE), Hot Springs, Arkansas.

"You're All Dead"

In mid-December 1969, the military detachment (supervised by civilians) conducted several weeks of night operations defending a small wooden pier on KMCAS. This was to prepare us for a major test of the dolphin's ability to defend a pier against a staged attack by Navy UDT/SEALs.

Their target was a short, low profile pier located next to a mangrove swamp, in the back east corner of KMCAS on Kaneohe Bay. A temporary office trailer located at the foot of the pier which served as our Operations Command Center (OPCON) became the SEALs' target. The UDT/SEALs were given the ground rules for the exercise test. They were to begin from some point in the bay or opposite shore and then swim with or without SCUBA and attack the pier and OPCON.

A Navy Commander from the CINCPACFLT staff was to be a neutral observer, who recorded significant events and submitted a report to his superior. When the Commander arrived that night, several of us noticed he was wearing a "Budweiser" (UDT/SEAL badge) but didn't think much of it at the time.

To defend the pier against the simulate attack by UDT/SEALs, we only had one prototype SVS and it was positioned at the head of this short pier. The dolphin could easily search 180 degrees out from the pier. I don't remember which dolphin was working that night (probably Slan, John or Toad).

The trainer began having the dolphin search for swimmers as darkness approached. The evening progressed without incident until a few hours after midnight.

Then all of a sudden the OPCON door was kicked open and there stood several UDT/SEALs pointing weapons at the watch standers. The SEALs simply said, "You're all dead."

This was a total surprise to everyone. How could this have happened? Our dolphin had not reported a single swimmer all night. This was one of our best dolphins who had detected countless swimmers over the past eighteen months during both day and night attacks coming from every possible angle.

At this point the OPCON watch standers could only wonder. How could our dolphin have missed not one but several swimmers?

Not a True "Swimmer" Attack

Later in the "Hot Wash-Up" (post-operation debriefing) we learned that all the UDT/SEALs had entered the bay from the opposite shoreline and swam in pairs (no SCUBA) to the swampy area, quite a distance to the east of the pier, and our OPCON. After reaching shore, they walked stealthily through the mangrove swamp until they reached the foot of the pier. Here they stopped, surveyed the area for a while, then charged into our OPCON.

Now we knew why the dolphin had not reported any swimmers. The UDT/SEALs did not conduct a true "swimmer attack" on the pier. They walked over land much of the way to reach our OPCON.

We could only assume the UDT/SEALs were misinformed or not properly briefed on the exercise rules and the purpose of this important test. They may have just been doing whatever it took to achieve the objective and take out the target. (My experiences working with SEALs later in my life, leads me to believe that the later was most likely the reason.) During the Hot Wash-up, someone pointed out that the dolphin was not able to search upland. This did not seem to make a difference; the UDT/SEALs had won. We were not comfortable with the test outcome, especially knowing that the test results would be reported to CINCPACFLT by an observer who was a Commander wearing a UDT/SEAL insignia.

All we could do now was wait to hear back what the CINCPAC observer reported to his superiors. The next week we learned that the CINCPAC observer did in fact conclude that the dolphin system had failed and "was not ready for operational deployment".

A Heavy Blow

Soon after that, Bill Powell received instructions from ONR's Bob Stone (STROMAC manager) to stop working on the dolphin swimmer defense system. We were to redirect resources towards developing other potential Navy applications for marine mammals.

This was a heavy blow to this close-knit group of professionals. Almost everyone had moved their families from California, left close friends, relatives and good jobs to work on this first-of-a-kind marine mammal system. This included managers, administrators, engineers, researchers, trainers, support staff and our small Navy military detachment. This was the end of a SECRET project that everyone had been totally dedicated to making successful. Up to this point, they had achieved every milestone and goal on, or ahead of, schedule. They had expended tremendous mental and physical energy and passion in accomplishing more than was expected.

Then someone proposed the only way to deal with this tragedy, was to hold a Wake. After all, we needed to acknowledge the unexpected death of this very important dolphin project.

The Wake was held the next weekend at the home of Hop Porter, MMP Engineering Div. Head. His house was in a residential development in Kailua called Enchanted Lakes where several other lab personnel lived, including Larry Phillips. Larry and I had decided the Wake needed an appropriate representative centerpiece.

So before the event, I went to Larry's, and we cut pieces of Styrofoam and assembled them into the shape of a dolphin. Next we covered and contoured this with paper-mache, then sprayed it with grey paint. After the paint dried, we took a photo of the dolphin symbolically being stabbed with a knife. We thought this an appropriate representation of our feelings surrounding the cancellation of our project, and how we reportedly "failed" the test against the UDT/SEALs.

Larry Phillips and Marty Conboy illustrate how the Navy killed the dolphin swimmer defense system, represented by the paper-mache dolphin at a "wake" held at Hop Porter's home, December 1969. *(Author's Photo, 1969.)*

The Wake was well attended. However, compared to other gatherings, such as new arrivals, Luaus, pumpkin-carving contests, weekend volleyball and sailing parties, this was definitely much more subdued. True, this group of professionals would soon gather their strength and move ahead and become equally dedicated to developing new and different marine mammal applications. But the project that had radically changed their lives was now dead... and the loss was difficult to overcome.

Everyone was trying to ignore the elephant in the room. Or in this case, the gray paper-mache dolphin. This was the end of the MMP's Swimmer Defense System — or was it?

III

REDIRECTION AND RESURRECTION

(1969-1970)

15

Redirection:
Quick Find, Deep Ops and
Sea Search/Linear Sweep;
Potential Marine Mammal Applications
(1969-1970)

A FTER THE WAKE FOR THE SWIMMER DEFENSE SYSTEM, marine mammal research changed significantly and was redirected toward other potential Navy applications. The Military Detachment trainers were re-assigned to various projects. Chief Bob Foster trained dolphins to locate and mark bottom mines for Larry Clark's Project Linear Sweep which evolved into possibly the Navy's most important systems (MK-7 and MK-8). This system was originally classified SECRET but later developed TOP SECRET capabilities. It was declassified in 1992.

Chief Gordon (Gordie) Sybrant learned how to train sea lions and worked with Marty Conboy's Project Quick Find. Senior Chief John Cirelli and my wife, Sharon, worked with Michael Greenwood's project; he was training dolphins to boat-follow for many miles at a time. Sharon worked at the Hanger 102 pier with a dolphin that was blind in one eye, training basic behaviors. When the sessions were over, she did volunteer work with Dr. John Allen, one of NUC Hawaii's veterinarians. Senior Chief Cirelli was not impressed with the project and was disappointed with the menial task he was assigned. The project was canceled in early 1970, and Greenwood was reassigned by Powell to write a Marine Mammal Training Manual. (See Appendix VII-B)

Sharon Goforth works at Hangar 102 with a dolphin that was blind in one eye, training basic behaviors for Michael Greenwood's project. *(Author's Photo, 1970.)*

Marine Mammal Technology

I continued my work as an editor, getting chapters written by our marine mammal experts. The chapters covered cetacean and sea lion natural and trained behaviors, capture, selection and transport of marine mammals. I contributed the introduction and a chapter on marine mammal taxonomy and terminology that included a short self-test. These chapters were later edited and published as Technical Report # 284, *An Introduction to Marine Mammal Technology, 1973.*

Sharon and I shared a large two-story home on the ocean in Lanikai, opposite the Mokulua Islands, with Dr. John Allen and Dr. Ross Pepper. I had assisted John Allen with several medical exams of dolphins and thought there may be a better way to strand and examine them.

So with help from engineers (Dan Hightower and Harry Chalmers), I installed an SVS pen floor on a standard floating pen. With the bottom raised, it could become a mobile medical pen. The pen's floor was a sturdy

Fiberglas grating and could be raised and lowered with a hand-winch with a set of cables and pulleys. The medical pen gate could be matched-up with the dolphin's pen gate, allowing the dolphin to be recalled into the medical pen. Once inside the medical pen, the gate was closed and the Fiberglas bottom raised-up so the medical staff could stand on it and maneuver the stranded dolphin into a stretcher. The stretcher sling was then connected to a davit, mounted on the pen walkway and the stretcher lifted. The davit was rotated, and stretcher poles lowered into four "U" brackets mounted waist-high on the walkway. Medical personnel could then easily walk around the dolphin, conduct examinations, take blood, urine and blowhole samples.

This greatly simplified physical exams and improved the safety for everyone (man and dolphin). There was only one problem. Using the medical pen required routine maintenance training of the dolphin. The dolphins quickly learned (as do most animals) that going into the medical pen may result in being stranded, poked, prodded and even stuck with a needle. To maintain this behavior, we matched the medical pen gate with the pen gate every few weeks and recalled the dolphin. This training included several trials without raising the pen bottom and the dolphin was richly rewarded. If we failed to conduct this maintenance training, the reliability degraded, but could be rapidly re-acquired.

Project Quick Find

Chief Gordon (Gordie) Sybrant and Jim Corey (hired in 1969 from the Aquatarium in St. Petersburg, Florida) became the primary sea lion trainers for Marty Conboy's object location and retrieval system (Project Quick Find). The project began in September 1969 and operated from the pier at Hanger 102. The pier had a large, fenced, covered kennel that housed six sea lions (Akahi, Fatman, Juneau, Turk, Sam and Sniffer). The kennel had a small fiberglass pool for cooling, and gated access to a 40 x 40-foot fenced swimming area. The Lab's engineering team constructed a specially designed pontoon boat for the project. It was outfitted with a 10 x 10-foot covered wheel house, a flat deck with a cradle for transporting Anti-Submarine Rocket (ASROC) shapes, a davit to lower and lift the shapes, several sea lion cages, and a small outboard rubber boat (Zodiac).

Hangar 102 pier with a covered sea lion kennel, a fenced swimming area, and the Quick Find boat. Quick Find's home. *(U.S. Navy. Used by permission.)*

Quick Find first demonstrated its operational capabilities on 6 November 1970, when it located and recovered a MK-17 ASROC depth charge on the bottom at 180 feet, near San Nicolas Island, California. Today, Quick Find is designated the MK-5 object recovery system. MK-5 animals also have been trained to recover dummy victims in a simulated airplane crash.[1]

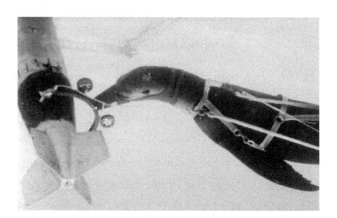

A sea lion practices underwater recovery of an object using a grabber device with a retrieval line. *(U.S. Navy, 1970. Used by permission.)*

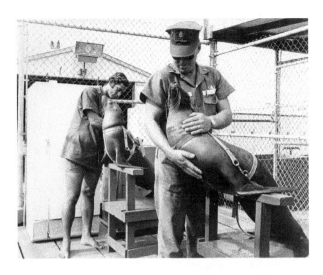

Jim Corey and Chief Gordie Sybrant harness Project Quick Find sea lions. *(U.S. Navy, 1970. Used by permission.)*

Larry Landis, Michael Schultz, and Gordie Sybrant training Quick Find sea lions to locate and recover objects. *(U.S. Navy. Used by permission.)*

Project Deep Ops

A few of the military men were assigned to Clark Bower's Project Deep Ops. They trained a Pacific pilot whale (*Globicephala macrorhynchus*) (Morgan), and two killer whales (*Orcinus orca*). The killer whale, Ahab, arrived in October 1969, and Ishmael, the other killer whale, arrived in January 1970. Deep Ops animals were trained to dive deeply, and mark and attach recovery devices on cylindrical objects. Having the whale enclosures at Sag Harbor, near the entrance to Kaneohe Bay, made it a short ride to very deep water.

Project Deep Ops pilot whale (Morgan) recovering object with grabber. *(U.S. Navy. Used by permission.)*

Project Deep Ops killer whale (Ahab) recovering object with grabber device.
(U.S. Navy, 1970. Used by permission.)

Deep Ops worked from the ocean-going boat (Luhrs) that Powell and Bowers had purchased when they first arrived in Hawaii (in late 1967-early 1968). They had originally planned to use it to study training wild dolphins in local Hawaiian waters. Pilot and killer whales had never been open-ocean released before this project, so they were initially trained in a large open pen at Sag Harbor, to establish reliable recall and boat-following behaviors.[2]

THOSE CREATIVE ENGINEERS:
NOVEL MARINE MAMMAL SYSTEMS HARDWARE DESIGN AND DEVELOPMENT

Every step of marine mammal training required our engineers to invent tools and equipment from scratch. No one had done before what we were doing, and we created it as we went. Here are a few key inventions.

Sentry Vehicle Station (SVS)

This novel and absolutely critical vessel could house a dolphin while anchored or traveling. The pontoons were purchased from Kyot, in Mankato, Minnesota, who built "party boats" designed for lakes. The SVS was designed by Doug Murphy and built by Harry Chalmers, Bob Flood, and Larry Phillips and others at NUC Hawaii (all originally from NOTS).

An SVS moored at OPCON Barge. Note: spotlight, pen opening in deck, folded net brackets, floatable anchor box and trainers' cabin. In the background is an underway SVS. *(Author's Photo, 1971.)*

Self-Contained Animal Transporter (SCAT)

The self-contained animal transporter (SCAT) was designed, built and patented in 1969 by Dan Hightower, Larry Phillips and Marty Conboy.

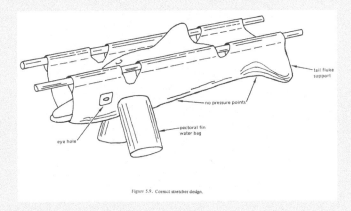

A 1969 line drawing of a modified dolphin transport stretcher (based on an original design from the Point Mugu Facility) used with the SCAT. *(U.S. Navy. Used by permission.)*

Larry Phillips and his dog, Tinker, in the KMCAS Hangar 102 with a SCAT, which Phillips co-invented and patented with Marty Conboy and Dan Hightower (1969).*(Courtesy of Larry Phillips, 1969.)*

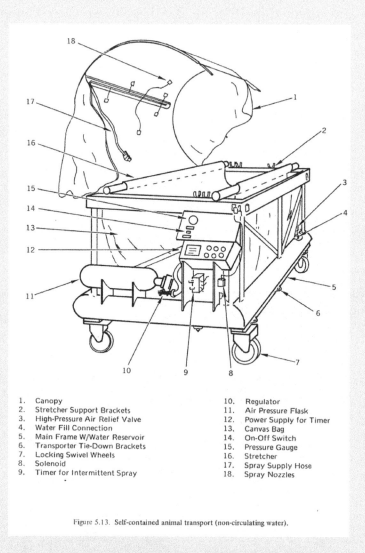

1.	Canopy	10.	Regulator
2.	Stretcher Support Brackets	11.	Air Pressure Flask
3.	High-Pressure Air Relief Valve	12.	Power Supply for Timer
4.	Water Fill Connection	13.	Canvas Bag
5.	Main Frame W/Water Reservoir	14.	On-Off Switch
6.	Transporter Tie-Down Brackets	15.	Pressure Gauge
7.	Locking Swivel Wheels	16.	Stretcher
8.	Solenoid	17.	Spray Supply Hose
9.	Timer for Intermittent Spray	18.	Spray Nozzles

Figure 5.13. Self-contained animal transport (non-circulating water).

A schematic of a SCAT (Self-Contained Animal Transporter) *(U.S. Navy. Used by permission.)*

(Courtesy of Dolores Powell, 1967.)

Bill Powell and Hop Porter on the tarmac near the boat shop at the Hawaii Lab, celebrating an engineering feat: the successful deployment of a helicopter transporter. It was designed to be used with a mine-hunting system, able to launch from shore or ship. One half of the transporter carried an inflatable boat. The other half contained a trained dolphin. The transporter was set down in the target area of the ocean, then the helo made a pass over the transporter, allowing the operators to jump into the water. They got the boat out, and then released the dolphin. Said Hop Porter: "The first test was from Kaneohe to a bay on the other side of Oahu, maybe Pokai Bay. When they opened the dolphin's enclosure, it backed out into the water as trained, took one look around and then jumped back into the transporter! It must have been a shock for the animal to jump into the transporter in one bay, then jump out in an entirely different bay. The trainers did coax the animal out and it did perform its task."

DIVERSIONS: IT WASN'T SCIENCE ALL THE TIME

NUC Hawaii had several sports teams that competed against other military teams on KMCAS. NUC fielded teams for indoor volleyball, fast-pitch softball and football (flag and tackle). During the fall 1969, NUC had a flag football team (called the Dolphins, of course) that did pretty well but no championship. In early 1970 NUC's indoor volleyball team went 12-0 and won the base championship. We didn't receive the award because we had too many civilians on the team. That spring the NUC softball team finished well, but short of a championship.

NUC flag football team, the Dolphins, 1969. Note: trainer Brooks Robbins w/broken hand. Front Row (L-R) D. McSheehy, L. Phillips, B. Robbins, R. Seiple, Jack Holzschue, R. Pepper, N. Estabrook. Back Row (L-R) Unknown, H. Goforth, J. Simons, M. Schultz, B. Steele, L. Landis and R. Buescher. *(U.S. Navy, 1969. Used by permission.)*

In 1970, for some unknown reason, the Marines replaced flag with tackle football. NUC's flag team members couldn't field a two-squad tackle team, but we found other Marine units with the same problem. So we joined with the Dispersing Department and the Brigg Police to make a full tackle team. The team was called the Dispo Dolphins, coached by the Dispersing Officer. I was the quarterback and the offensive line was made up of Tom Peeling (center); Bill Steele, Don McSheehy (tackles); Jim Corey and another fellow (guards); Norm Chun and John Barnes (running backs); Larry Landis, Mike Schultz and Bill McCain (ends). McCain had played for Mississippi State. The defensive squad was headed by a fellow who played linebacker at West Virginia, and his defensive line was mostly muscular Samoans from the Brigg Police.

16

Birth of Short Time:
Powell Tells Zumwalt We Can Be Ready
in Ninety Days
(Late September 1970)

ADMIRAL ELMO R. (BUD) ZUMWALT WAS NOMINATED BY President Nixon to be the Chief of the Naval Operations (CNO) on 14 April, 1970. He left Vietnam in May and officially became the CNO on 1 July. During his first few weeks as CNO, he was occupied dealing with several difficult international issues; deploying carrier task groups to the Mediterranean to prevent the collapse of a ninety-day cease-fire between Israel and Egypt; preparing for the second round of Strategic Arms Limitations Talks (SALT); unrest between Palestinian commandos and the Jordanian government; and the continuing Vietnam truce negotiations in Paris.

Admiral Elmo R. (Bud) Zumwalt (now CNO) orders that Project Short Time be resurrected and deployed to Vietnam. *(U.S. Navy. Used by permission.)*

In spite of all this, Zumwalt scheduled a meeting in late September to be briefed by the heads of Naval Research and Development programs. They included Bob Stone (OP-987), the head of Project STROMAC, which sponsored the Navy's marine mammal programs.

In 1969, while at COMNAVFORV, Zumwalt had learned that a swimmer defense system using dolphins was being developed. Now, at the Pentagon, Zumwalt asked Stone if the dolphin system was ready yet. Stone told him that it actually had been ready in December 1969, and could be made ready again.

"How long will it take to get this to Vietnam?" Zumwalt asked. "I want it there as soon as possible."

"I'll have to call the Project Manager, Bill Powell, to find out," Stone replied.

This would be the first in a chain of phone calls, ending with a miscommunication that became the reason for the new name of this resurrected project.

No Turning Back

Stone excused himself to call Powell at NUC Hawaii.

Powell told Stone that the timetable for the project depended on how long it would take to build three sentry vehicle stations (SVS), the special boats that the dolphins worked in. Powell said he would find out and call back as soon as possible. Then he dialed Hop Porter, the Engineering Division Head for the Marine Mammal Program at the Hawaii Lab.

Porter still had the original design plans for the prototype SVS that had been used with the dolphins to evaluate the swimmer defense system for more than a year. He quickly contacted the contractor who had built the prototype boat in 1968, who estimated it would take ninety days to make the three SVSs after receiving an approved, signed contract.

Several times over the next forty-plus years, Porter and Powell would joke about exactly what Hop *said* and what Bill *heard* in the conversation that followed.

Those familiar with the federal government know that because of the labyrinth of rules and regulations, it takes a sizeable amount of time (two to six months) to "let a contract". The government agency writes a Statement of Work, advertises a Request for Proposal from potential contractors, performs a review and grading of the proposals, and finally writes and sends the contract to the contractor for signatures. Only after all this is completed, can any government contract "be let".

Porter called Powell back. "Bill, the three SVSs can be ready ninety days after the contract is let."

Powell immediately called Stone and told him, "The swimmer defense system can be ready in ninety days." Stone in turn informed Admiral Zumwalt.

There was no turning back now.

The next day, Powell saw Porter at the office and said how pleased he was that this project was not only being resurrected but would be in Vietnam in ninety days.

Porter looked at Powell in unbelief. "Bill, I told you that the contractor could deliver the SVS boats ninety days after *the contract is let*, not ninety days from today!"

Now they had a problem.

Meeting the Deadline

Thus Project Short Time was born. Because of a little miscommunication, they had only a *short time* to get the job done which thus became the project's name.

The Hawaii Lab's military and civilians were faced with three months to return the swimmer defense system to its full, effective, operational condition. Not only did they have to build three SVS boats, they had to order in and train additional military personnel to become dolphin trainers, and retrain the original five dolphins, Garth, John, Slan, Tinker and Toad.

Porter went to work immediately to solve the SVS construction problem. He called his boss, Howard Talkington, in San Diego and explained the problem. Talkington told Porter to call Art Schlosser at the San Diego, Naval Undersea Center, Ocean Engineering Division, and see if he could help.

The good news was that when Porter called and told Schlosser that he already had the SVS design plans, Schlosser said he could make and deliver the SVSs in the required ninety days.

As it turned out, during the later stages of SVS construction, Schlosser said he might need more funding to make sure he would meet the deadline. Powell somehow came up with the extra money, but in the end, Schlosser never used it.

Porter next ordered his Special Projects "go-to guy", Larry Phillips, to fly to the mainland and get a contract with the Kayot Company, maker of the aluminum pontoons that the SVSs were constructed on. Each SVS required a pair of pontoons, so the project needed six right away.

The next day Phillips jetted to California and met with a Kayot representative. He had with him Project Short Time's Priority-1 ("Brickbat"), the highest purchasing authority in the Naval Supply System. This made it possible to complete the contract on the spot that day. In less than twenty-four hours, six pontoons were express-shipped from the Kayot headquarters in Minnesota to Art Schlosser at NUC San Diego.

With everyone working hard and overtime, the SVS boats arrived at NUC Hawaii on time.

Now the next challenge: To conduct the historic deployment of the Defender dolphins to Vietnam.

THE NAVY'S THIRD MARINE MAMMAL OFFICER COMES ON BOARD
(SEPTEMBER-OCTOBER 1970)

Up to this point Lt. Dave Ussery, the senior officer of the NUC Marine Mammal Detachment, had selected all the EOD personnel who were assigned to our detachment. For some reason, Bill Powell asked if I would like to select the third EOD officer for Project Short Time. He said I would have only one opportunity.

My first thought was to call Ltjg. Rick Fischer at EODGRULANT where I had worked in the Operations Department eighteen months earlier. After college, Rick had decided to join the Navy, and volunteered for EOD School. During the summer of 1967, we were in the same class at Underwater Swimmers School in Key West. That summer Rick became very interested in collecting tropical fish. He befriended a local fish collector, Billy Causey, living on Big Pine Key, who taught him many fish collecting techniques. Rick and I had also been on the Navy EOD volleyball team that won the Fort Story Army Base Championship.[1]

Rick had already served a tour as O-in-C of an EOD Detachment in Da Nang, Vietnam. At that time, this made Rick one of the few East Coast EOD Officers to get an assignment to Vietnam. Clearly, his recent in-country experience and strong interest in marine life would be perfect for Project Short Time. Since Powell had said I could only make one call, Rick was my obvious first choice.

So that evening about midnight in late September 1970, I dialed "O" for operator assistance to place a person-to-person call from my home. I knew this would be expensive, but I didn't care, this was a very important call. The operator introduced herself as Mary and was quite friendly and helpful. I told her I needed to call an EOD Officer named Rick Fischer on the East Coast but didn't have his home phone number nor the number for the EODGRULANT Quarterdeck.

It was a small coincidence that her boyfriend was an EOD Officer.[2] I didn't know him. Mary navigated her way to the EODGRULANT Quarterdeck and got through to the Command Duty Officer (CDO). She was successfully persuasive in her request for Rick's home phone number, which turned out to be the EOD junior officer's beach cottage in Virginia Beach, Virginia. Mary placed the call.

They were all sound asleep but someone close to the phone answered, and Mary said, "Hal Goforth is calling from Hawaii for Rick Fischer." The phone was passed to Rick who managed to say, "Hello Hal, what's up?"

I apologized for calling so early, and told him as much as I could about this opportunity and why I thought it would be a perfect fit for him. Rick thanked me for thinking of him, but said, "Hal, I just landed the O-in-C billet at the Key West EOD Detachment and you know how much I wanted that!"

I did know. Happy for him, but disappointed for me, I asked if he knew anyone else who may be interested. Rick called out, "Anyone interested in a billet in Hawaii?"

Les Bivens was awake enough to answer "Yes!" Rick passed him the phone. After I repeated what I had said to Rick, Les said it sounded good to him.

No one at the command had ever seen orders cut so fast. The man who would be the Navy's third marine mammal officer arrived at the NUC Hawaii Lab twelve days later. He, and eight enlisted personnel, arrived and began learning to train, operate, and care for the five dolphins that would soon defend the tri-service ammo pier at Cam Ranh Bay.

17

Deploying the Defender Dolphins:
The Move to Vietnam
(December 1970)

O N 17 DECEMBER 1970, I STOOD ON THE TARMAC AT Kaneohe Marine Corps Air Station, and watched thirteen men from my unit load five dolphins into a mammoth C-141 cargo plane and take off without me.

It had been exactly one year since we held the wake after the demise of the swimmer defense system. Now, because Admiral Zumwalt was the CNO, this system was on its way to Vietnam. And I wasn't. At least not yet.

I wondered why I had felt so alone and abandoned at that moment. Maybe it was because I had been the first military person to join this project back in May 1969. I had made my first swim against these dolphins during a simulated deployment to Key West. I had worked closely with the NUC civilian trainers, scientists and veterinarians to develop a marine mammal training course (complete with a booklet, lectures, written and practical exams) that all Short Time personnel took and passed. The day Short Time was born, Bill Powell told me to go work with Clark Bowers and learn the steps required to train a dolphin to perform the complete chain of behaviors for swimmer detection and marking. "I want at least one military person to know how these dolphins were originally trained," he said.

For a year and a half, Short Time had been my *raison d'être*. Now I could only watch the big gray plane roar down the long runway towards the ocean, slowly climb into the clear blue Hawaiian sky and make a sweeping turn to the west. But the reason I wasn't on that plane was a positive one. My wife, Sharon, and I are grateful to this day to Lt. Les Bivens for taking my place so that I could delay my deployment to be present for the birth of our first child, Kendra Joanne. She was due 21 December but would be delivered 2 January 1971.

Even anticipating that happy event, I regretted not sharing my unit's experiences in the early days. I stood looking at the plane as it got smaller and smaller feeling strangely disconnected.

It would be a full day later before the Animal Flight with Bivens, TD-1 Bill Scronce, MNC Dick Pence, MMC Gordon Sybrant, GMC Bob Foster, HMC Jim Bush, GMG-1 Dave Hart, TM-2 Jack Brown, AO-1 Willie Roebuck, TM-2 Dave Walsh, SM-2 Charlie Wongdock, BM-1 Art Turnbough and OTSN Mike Bragget would disembark and begin to make Powell and Woody's Advanced Development Plan a reality. It would be twenty-four hours before five uniquely trained dolphins would be able to swim again in their enclosures at Market Time Cove in Cam Ranh Bay.

How would it all turn out?

Heading to Cam Ranh Bay

It had been a crushing ninety days of preparation. For the prior eight months, Short Time's dolphins had been working on other behaviors (e.g., echolocation studies, bottom mine location and marking, etc). Garth, John, Slan, Tinker and Toad needed "refresher training" in swimmer detection and marking. Through the dedicated efforts of civilian and military trainers, all the dolphins returned to high levels of performance in less than three months.

Art Schlosser and his Engineering Department at NUC San Diego had completed the three new SVSs and flown them to the Hawaii Lab. Special Projects manager Larry Phillips (armed with a Priority 1) had outfitted the team with a wide variety of tools, outboard motors, equipment and critical system components. This included twenty individually-fitted, marking nose cups, four for each dolphin made by a company outside of Philadelphia, Pennsylvania.

The new EOD personnel who joined Project Short Time in September completed extensive classroom and practical training and were now proficient at operating every aspect of the dolphin swimmer defense system. In November, Bill Scronce, one of the first (and unquestionably the most experienced) Navy dolphin trainers, joined Short Time and became head of the military trainers. Bill had been at the Naval Air Technical Training "B" School in Millington, Tennessee, to become eligible for Chief, but before graduating, he left to join us and delayed his well deserved advancement. We had worked as a team for several months and conducted several weeks of all night operations in preparation for Vietnam.

The deployment site for Project Short Time had to be chosen carefully. In October that year, Powell, Phillips, and Scott Johnson visited three high-value sites in Vietnam suggested by Admiral Zumwalt. These were Sea Float in the Cau Long River, the Naval Support Facility on the Cua Viet River, near the DMZ, and Cam Ranh Bay (CRB). CRB's ammunition pier was the only site with an environment that the swimmer defense system, as currently designed, could operate effectively.

Project Short Time's official military unit designation was Coastal Task Unit (CTU) 115.9.1, which operated at CRB's ammo pier with living quarters and offices five miles away at Market Time Cove.

On 16 December 1970, the day before the Animal Flight took off, Phillips, Milo McManus, Marty Conboy, and Marine Mammal Detachment Officer-in-Charge Lt. Dave Ussery, flew to Saigon on a military contract flight. They spent a night at the Saigon EOD Detachment "Villa", and the next day flew to Cam Ranh Bay on a C-7A Caribou where they waited for the Animal Flight to arrive.

Equipment and Facilities

Before the dolphins and men arrived, all the support equipment had to be shipped, and the facilities prepared.

In late November 1970, a team of Project Short Time's civilians loaded a C-141 at Kaneohe Marine Corps Air Station bound for CRB. The Equipment Flight would transport three new SVSs on trailers, two modified Boston Whalers on trailers, modular components for five dolphin enclosures, a walk-in fish freezer, two spare Homelite outboards, a mechanic's "dream set" of tools, spare parts, and more.

In preparation for the Short Time equipment flight from Hawaii to Cam Ranh Bay, SVSs are loaded into an Air Force C-141. *(U.S. Navy. Used by permission.)*

Bill Powell (left) and Marty Conboy during load-out of equipment for flight from KMCAS. In rear, Dave Ussery (right) and John Cirell. *(Author's Photo, 1970.)*

Two days earlier, Bill Steele and his "marines" (Pete Makalii, Paul Jones, Rick Kahakina, and Adam Camara) flew ahead on a military contract flight to Saigon. They too spent a night in Saigon at the EOD Detachment's "Villa" and the next day caught a flight on a C-7A Caribou to the CRB Air Force Base. Later that afternoon, Steele and his men met the Equipment Flight and with the help of Naval Construction Battalion Maintenance Unit 302, offloaded its cargo.

Steele had nothing but highest praise for these Seabees. As their creed says, *The man who says it can't be done, usually finds himself being interrupted by a CBMU 302 Seabee doing it.* The Seabees' expert assistance continued for two weeks. Together they constructed concrete slabs, partitioned and outfitted Quonsets huts, set up workshops, assembled dolphin enclosures, secured the fish freezer and trailers to slabs, set up the fish preparation area, and much more.

Completing this infrastructure was absolutely essential before men and dolphins arrived late on the night of 18 December.

Weather and the War Zone

How do you make a dolphin fly? In a self-contained animal transporter (SCAT). (See sidebar Chapter 15: "Those Creative Engineers: Novel Marine Mammal Systems Hardware Design and Development.")

It was well into the night of 18 December when the Animal Flight landed at the CRB Air Force Base after stops for fuel on Wake Island, U.S. Territory, and at Air Force Base at Kadena, Okinawa.

The monsoon season in this part of Vietnam runs from October to mid-January. During monsoons, rainfall averages eight to ten inches a month, and winds, with peak gusts, can reach 26-47 mph. It was under these conditions that the Animal Flight landed. It was pitch black. Unrelenting heavy rain was falling, with strong winds blowing constantly. It took over an hour to offload the five dolphins in SCATs, and other cargo into trucks.

Because of the conditions, it took two hours to drive the fifteen miles to Market Time Cove at the southern end of the peninsula. Scronce remembers vividly that just as they were driving off the airfield, alarms sounded. People were running to General Quarters as helicopters took off and artillery guns began firing across the bay into the distant mountainside. This action lasted the entire truck ride to Market Time.

"What the hell am I doing here?" Scronce recalls thinking.

Tracers coming from the 20mm mini-gun pods on AH-1 Cobra helos looked like a dragon's tongue reaching out and touching the land across the bay. Scronce was jolted into realizing that he was now in a war zone.

Definitely not in Kansas or Kaneohe anymore.

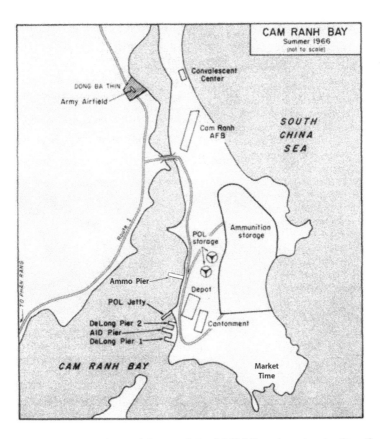

Map of Cam Ranh Bay adapted from original 1966 line drawing by Ray Smith. Used by permission. Note the distance from the CRB AFB where Short Time landed, to Market Time at the southern-most point, and from Market Time to the ammo pier.

Stiff but Safe

Arriving at Market Time Cove after midnight, the men carefully hoisted Garth, John, Slan, Tinker, and Toad in their stretchers out of the SCATs and released them into individual floating pens moored to the western quay wall.

The dolphins were stiff from using unconditioned muscles to breathe in a gravity environment. Aquatic mammals don't experience gravity in water. Imagine having to lie flat on your chest with hands behind you back and breathing in this position for twenty-four hours against gravity. Consider also that prior to this you lived 99 percent of your life in a weightless environment. (Aquatic living is so similar to weightlessness that astronauts practice performing tasks in swimming pools to simulate weightless conditions. Before returning to earth they must perform exercises in space to prepare to walk normally upon returning to our 1 G environment.)

The men too were stiff and bone tired from the long flight. Still, in the dark, rainy night, they got down into the pens and supported each dolphin for a few minutes until it could swim on its own normally. A four-hour watch section was set to carefully monitor their behavior throughout this first night. They were dauntlessly taking on a new adventure — in the teeth of a monsoon.

Project Short Time had arrived.

IV

ROUGH SEAS

(1971)

18

Monsoons and Other Troubles: Early Days and Problems Setting Up at Cam Ranh Bay (18-27 December 1970)

O N 20 DECEMBER 1971, AFTER THE DOLPHINS HAD spent two days in pens moored at the Market Time quay wall, the team moved them to a more protected site behind a small island just outside Market Time Cove. This site was much better protected from the strong northeast winds. Bad weather continued, making it too risky to attempt towing the dolphins eight miles north to the Operations Control (OPCON) barge.

On 22 December, with the monsoon at full force, the military trainers, led by Bill Scronce and Bob Foster, trained all five dolphins in the lee of the small island. At the same time, some of the men worked at making the Quonset huts more livable, while others installed electricity and outfitted the OPCON barge.

Cargo ships at Cam Ranh Bay Ammo Pier, 1971.*(Author's Photo, 1971.)*

This large barge had previously served as the operations base for a Water Dog swimmer detection unit. The unit apparently had not worked well here or at Sea Float, due to the presence of engine exhausts, wind, and rain, which had interfered with the Water Dog's effectiveness. This barge was ideal for Short Time. It was secured to several clusters of large pilings, and was located approximately half a mile south of the ammunition pier.

This ammo pier was a definitely a high-value swimmer sapper target. A massive amount of ordnance was off-loaded 24/7 from cargo ships. The ordnance and supplies were simultaneously loaded onto Army trucks working in a conga line on the pier. During the previous year, in 1970, Cam Ranh Bay was the busiest port in Southeast Asia, off-loading more than 600,000 short tons from deep draft Sea-Land cargo ships, barges, and other vessels. CRB averaged 42 ships per month and off-loaded 28,000 short tons and 29 million gallons of petroleum, oil and lubricants (POL) per month. The Army's 124th Transportation Command convoys (566th, 592nd, and 670th Companies) loaded with ammunition and supplies, averaged 10 long hauls and 60 short hauls per month from CRB to in-country military units.

Bill Scronce recalls only seven days during the year that Short Time was in CRB, that a ship was not at the ammo pier and needed protection from swimmer sappers.

Toad's Scratched Corneas

Garth, John, Slan, and Tinker had come through the long flight from Hawaii to Vietnam quite well. Toad, however, had badly scratched the cornea of both eyes. She struggled frequently in her stretcher and had to be restrained with well-padded straps. However, this did not prevent her from raising and lowering her head often during the long flight.

After she was placed in her pen at Market Time, HMC Bush, serving as a veterinary technician, provided medical care and applied drops daily to her eyes. (When I arrived on 10 February, I brought with me special eye drops provided by one of NUC's vets, Dr. John Allen. They were to prevent permanent eye damage. I applied the solution two times a day for several weeks but unfortunately her cloudy corneas never cleared. It was impossible to keep the drops in her eyes very long, because she was an aquatic mammal. Dr. Allen later told me that because it had been a month since she damaged her corneas, it was probably too late for the drops to be effective.)

On 23 December, Bill, and Milo McManus decided to conduct a training session behind the island with Toad to see if her eye problems affected her trained behaviors. The session went smoothly and Toad performed well at this temporary site. However, later when Short Time moved and began operating at the ammo pier, Toad avoided swimming near seawalls, pilings, and under the pier. Fortunately, after a month at the ammo pier, Toad had adapted and would swim anywhere. For the next forty-plus years, her impaired vision never affected her swimmer defense performance at all.

The next day was Christmas Eve. Bill and Milo trained John and Toad behind the small island, despite the relentless rain and wind. Bad weather or not, Lt. Dave Ussery was under pressure from the head of the Coastal Task Group (CTG) and IUWG-1 Harbor Defense to have the dolphin system operating at the ammo pier by Christmas.

Moving the dolphins and pens to the OPCON barge would prove a huge challenge, perhaps contributing to Short Time's first major setback.

19

Merry Christmas and Welcome to Vietnam; A Dangerous Move for Man and Dolphins (25 December 1970)

O N CHRISTMAS DAY, IN STEADY WIND AND RAIN, Short Time team members used a MIKE-8 boat to tow the five dolphins in their floating pens from the small island near Market Time Cove to the OPCON barge. Bill Scronce and Milo McManus remember this operation being extremely difficult and quite dangerous.

The MIKE-8 was driven using only one of its two engines and at its slowest possible speed. Nevertheless, due to the strong current from the prop wash, the dolphins could not face forward in their pens and instead swam in circles. Many times the prop wash pushed a dolphin sideways and pinned it against the netting of the pen. Several times the men had to stop the MIKE-8, jump into a pen, and get a dolphin out of the net. To make matters worse, twice a pen broke loose from its tow-line and had to be retrieved and reattached.

With all these problems, the trip took several hours to travel approximately eight miles to the OPCON barge. After arriving, the pens were secured to the leeward side of the barge. Since it was too rough to begin nighttime operations, Boatswain's Mate Art Turnbough was left on the barge to stand night watch with a 22-foot Boston Whaler. Turnbough was selected because boatswain's mates are noted for their knot-tying skills and are considered the Navy's senior enlisted rating.

The barge was half-covered with a corrugated metal roof and a large, unpartitioned, walled area. Here was a desk, several chairs, one citizen band and multiple military radios, a mini-weather station, maps, charts, moon phase and current tables, tide plots, coffee maker, hot plate, soup pot, pantry with military rations, weapons rack, two bunks, logbooks, animal performance records and a few foot lockers. At the far end of the barge away from the animal pens, was a Porta Potty mounted over the water.

Bill Scronce checks tide, wind conditions, and moon charts at the OPCON Watch Desk. Note multiple radios, logbooks, and mini weather station. *(Author's Photo, 1971.)*

Gone Missing

The next morning, Turnbough awoke and was shocked to find that during the night our Whaler had broken loose and drifted away. The wind had been blowing consistently from the northeast towards an unfriendly shoreline to the southwest. The boat was absolutely necessary for the unit to function properly and had to be found. So, AO-1 Willie Roebuck and OTSN Mike Bragget, plus Milo McManus, our civilian technical representative, took the remaining Whaler to look for the lost boat.

They crossed the bay and drove several miles downwind, surveying the southwestern shoreline with binoculars. Finally they saw what looked like a boat wedged in the rocks along the shore. When they got closer they could tell that it was the Short Time boat, but it appeared damaged and would have to be towed home. The rocks along the shore made it impossible to drive close enough to tie a line to the boat, so Willie devised a plan. Milo would drive the Whaler, and Willie would get in the water with a long rope and go attach it to the boat's bow. Mike would take Willie's CAR-15, wade ashore and stand guard on the ridge overlooking the area while Willie and Milo prepared the Whaler for towing.

Except for our corpsmen, Mike was one of two Short Time sailors who were not EOD technicians. Mike had been studying to become an Ocean Systems Technician (OT) and someone in the NUC San Diego Personnel Department thought he'd be a good match for Short Time. He had absolutely no experience with weapons.

Reluctantly, Mike took the CAR-15 and began wading ashore. Willie didn't know much about him and yelled, "Bragget, what are you going to do if you see someone?"

Mike yelled back, "I don't know. I don't how to shoot!"

Luck was with them. No bad guys showed up during the boat recovery operation. Willie secured the damaged boat and tied it to the Whaler, which Milo drove directly to Market Time. Luckily, Mike returned without having to fire a shot. The boat was later repaired by Chiefs Gordie Sybrant and Bob Foster, our boat and motor experts.

The OPCON Chase Boat, a modified 18-foot Whaler with a 150hp outboard. Note the handheld spotlight for night searches. *(Author's Photo, 1971.)*

DODGING "FRIENDLY FIRE"
(JANUARY 1971)

In January 1971, before I arrived in CRB, something occurred during a simulated swimmer attack that might have lost us our Officer-in-Charge, and changed procedures from that day forward.

Normally, every night at dusk and often at pre-dawn, OPCON personnel took a Whaler and dropped off a swimmer outside the dolphin's detection range. The swimmer would hang on a channel buoy or tread water for a while and then swim slowly and quietly towards the ship or pier simulating a sapper. Normally, only one swimmer made the simulated attack, but occasionally there were two. Because the dolphins quickly learned to track the boat and search for the entry of possible swimmers, the boat maneuvered to confuse them by making several large sweeping passes across the search zones of all three dolphins on station. The boat was also driven over the same course several times during the night when OPCON personnel delivered hot coffee or soup to the SVS operators.

In addition to the dolphin, the swimmer was always up against several security forces: the Army sentry in a tower at the head of the pier, Army sentries on the ships, Harbor Patrol boats with a Vietnamese crew and U.S. Advisor, inadvertent attack helicopter fly-bys, and (during the first weeks) VNN Patrol boats with no U.S. Advisors.

One day before dawn, Dave Ussery prepared to swim against one of the dolphins. He decided to enter the water from shore instead of from a boat, so he had Dave Hart drive him north of the pier and drop him off along the shoreline. Ussery, wearing only swim trunks and carrying his fins, made his way across a sand bar that jutted into the bay.

Just before reaching the water he heard an M-16 firing from the guard tower and rounds hitting nearby. Ussery instinctively flattened and remained motionless on the sand waiting for the shooting to stop. Hart had heard the firing and drove full throttle to the guard tower. He leaped out of the jeep, ran towards the tower screaming, and scrambled up the ladder. The guard had stopped firing but this made no difference to Hart. Hart gave him more than an earful. When he had finished venting, he drove back to pick up Ussery.

When he pulled up, he found a very pissed-off lieutenant who told him to drive him straight to the tower. It was now Ussery's turn to educate the guard. Then he and Hart visited the remaining sentries. After this experience, Ussery made only a few swims, but ... this would not be his last encounter with sentries in the tower.

ASLEEP ON WATCH

Immediately the Standard Operating Procedures (SOP) were changed to require that before any simulated swimmer attack, an OPCON watch-stander would have a face-to-face talk with the sentry in the tower, and those on each cargo ship. At times there were several guards to visit, including those stationed on the outboard side of each ship, and one in the watch tower. Following the new SOP several weeks later, at dawn, Ussery climbed the guard tower ladder to visit the sentry only to find him asleep with his weapon leaning in a corner. This was, especially in a war zone, at minimum a court-martial offense.[1]

The last thing we needed was for a guard to wake up and see our swimmer and start firing. To make a lasting impact on the guard, he quietly took the sentry's M-16 rifle and climbed down the ladder. That morning we didn't have to worry about this guard firing at our swimmer. As usual, after the swimmer attack, our night time duty was over. The men secured the SVSs to the barge, put the dolphins in their pens, and set the daytime watch. We got in our Whaler, drove to shore, piled into our truck and rode to the Ville. Here we picked up our housekeeper, Lum, and drove back to Market Time. This was our daily routine, except today we had an extra M-16.

Lt. Ussery soon learned that he had made his point with the Army unit that supplied the sentries. A Colonel who was the Commanding Officer of the Army's 124th Transportation Command called our unit and instructed Ussery to bring him the M-16, ASAP. Ussery, not one easily intimidated, waited several days before "he found time" to visit the Colonel. Their meeting resulted in a standoff, the Colonel adamantly insisting Ussery could not take a weapon from a guard in a war zone, and Ussery unwavering in his insistence that the guard was sleeping on watch in a war zone and in clear violation of Article 113.

Lt. Chris Frier recalls that after I left Vietnam in May, this happened four more times before Short Time left in December 1971. Each time they took their sweet time before returning the weapon to the Colonel.

20

One Dolphin Goes AWOL: Why Did Tinker Leave? (27 December 1971)

TWO DAYS AFTER THE ANIMALS HAD BEEN TOWED TO the OPCON barge in their pens, Tinker was being trained near the ammo pier by Milo and Bill. She was in an SVS and performing her searches while one of our men was simulating a swimmer attack. Tinker detected and reported the swimmer and confirmed her response. Bill placed the nosecup on her rostrum and opened the gate and released her to mark the swimmer. She swam out of the SVS in the direction of the swimmer, but she never returned.

Immediately, the Short Time Whalers and SVSs were underway searching the area and rest of the bay. Each boat had a recall pinger and a few fish. Days later, Les Bivens learned that the day after Tinker left, a Vietnamese Harbor Patrol boat had seen a dolphin swimming in the bay not far from the pier. Unfortunately, Short Time was not notified until it was much too late to do anything. Tinker's nosecup was later found near the pier, so she apparently tossed it off as she swam away.

Helicopters and Short Time boats searched the bay for four days to no avail. Tinker was never again seen by Short Time personnel.

Losing Tinker caused great concern that other dolphins might be lost as well. This led to a new procedure designed to reduce the chances of losing another dolphin. There was pressure on Lt. Dave Ussery from Joint Defense Operations Center (JDOC) to begin operating at the pier, which produced a degree of stress. The weather was still not cooperating.

Ussery told the trainers to stop the practice of boat-following to duty stations and to transport dolphins everywhere inside the SVS pen. Clark Bowers had already returned to Hawaii when he learned about the loss of Tinker and doesn't remember recommending this procedure to Ussery. I arrived a month later and found the new procedure still in effect.

Why Did Tinker Leave?

Tinker was lost in the daytime on 27 December. It was during one of her first training sessions at the ammo pier and her first chance to swim freely since arriving at the OPCON barge. Only two days earlier, she had been towed behind a MIKE-8 for four hours in rough seas and exposed to strong propeller wash.

After the long tow trip, her floating pen was moored to the OPCON barge along with the other dolphins. Since arriving in CRB she had always been transported to her work and training stations inside an SVS pen. To do this, the trainers matched the SVS gate to the gate on the dolphin's pen and called the dolphin into the SVS pen with a pinger. The SVS was then driven to the station for a training session or night duty. This procedure was reversed when the session was over.

This procedure eliminated free-swimming by the dolphin. These dolphins had never been restricted like this before. This was not an appropriate way to treat dolphins that had enjoyed years with regular, daily free-swimming opportunities. Also, this was not how the system had been designed, trained and operated by the civilians and military trainers for the past few years. When I arrived 13 February, my first challenge was to change this restrictive procedure to avoid losing any more dolphins.

In an attempt to understand what caused Tinker to leave, some thought that moving the dolphins from Hawaii to a new and strange environment may have confused them and disrupted performance behaviors. However, the Technical Evaluation test, conducted in May 1969 at Key West with the same five dolphins suggests this was not the problem. The Technical Evaluation found that after flying from Hawaii to Key West, they immediately adapted to the unfamiliar Key West waters and performed all behaviors perfectly. I knew this from personal observations, because I swam against these same five dolphins several times during that test.

The big difference was, unlike Key West, Cam Ranh Bay had VNN patrol boats that randomly tossed concussion grenades in the water not far from the dolphin pens all night. Dolphins are highly acoustic animals and quite sensitive to loud sounds. It is the opinion of many scientists and trainers that a combination of factors (such as a strange environment, a four-hour long, rough tow in a pen, grenade explosions combined with restricted free-swimming opportunities) all had stressed Tinker beyond her tolerance level.

For two days and nights before she left, Tinker had been exposed to these random grenade explosions. After moving to the OPCON barge, Lt. Ussery and Ltjg. Bivens had gone to the Harbor Defense Headquarters (IUWG-1) and insisted this activity be stopped immediately.

Unfortunately, only the VNN patrol boats that had a U.S. Advisor on-board complied.

After Tinker went AWOL, Ussery returned to IUWG-1, and this time demanded an end to the practice of tossing grenades anywhere near the pier. This time all VNN patrol boats were ordered, by higher authority, to remain at least 2,000 meters from the OPCON barge and Ammo pier.

Unfortunately, by this time the horse (the dolphin) was already out of the barn.

Luckily, the remaining four dolphins never failed to return from a free-swimming session during the next eleven-months at Cam Ranh Bay.

V

PROJECT SHORT TIME IN ACTION

(1971)

21

In Country:
Reconnecting with the Team
(12 February 1971)

EIGHT WEEKS AFTER I WATCHED THE PROJECT SHORT
Time team and five dolphins take off from Kaneohe Marine Corps Air
Station without me, and a month after my first child was born, I flew to
Vietnam.

On 7 February I flew from Hickam Air Force Base to Saigon's Tan Son
Nhut Air Force Base. At the arrival terminal, an EOD officer from the Saigon
EOD Detachment greeted me and drove me in his jeep to check in at the
NAVFORV Command.

There I picked up my government issued clothing, shoes, weapons, back-
pack, lightweight blanket, and so on. Since I was an officer, in addition to a
CAR-15 rifle I was issued an M1911 Colt .45 pistol. Then we drove to the
EOD "Villa", where he showed me my rack, complete with mosquito netting.
I dropped my bags on the bunk and was given a tour of the two-story con-
crete building.

In the rooftop bar, my guide pointed out several bullet holes in the
wall behind the bar. Apparently, the music had been too loud the previous
Saturday night. Someone (perhaps the Viet Cong?) in a nearby building had
fired several rounds at the revelers. This was not reassuring.

I already felt uneasy riding in an unprotected jeep around a city at war.
Saigon was overflowing with Vietnamese walking and riding the streets,
crammed with Vespa and Lambretta scooters, bikes, small cars and minibus-
es. I had received the required pre-deployment training at EODTRAPAC's

"VC village" at West Loch, Oahu and learned Viet Cong used bikes and scooters to kill and maim.

Despite my apprehension, since I had only one night in Saigon, I accepted an invitation to venture into the city and experience its culture. Before leaving the EOD Villa, I was told to remove my officer and EOD insignias. I remember little of what I saw. However I remember constantly surveying the establishments' patrons and checking exits and entrances. I don't believe I appeared paranoid, but I engaged in little conversation (and my friends all know this was very atypical). Still, while sitting at the bar sipping Tiger and Ba Mui Ba ("33") beer, more than one Vietnamese "lady" came up, placed her hand on my thigh, and said, "GI, you numba one, you buy me drink!"

After several bars, we returned to the EOD Villa where a Vietnamese Army guard let us through the gate. I told myself he had to have been properly investigated, and was on our side. Before going to bed I took my second dose of quinine pills for malaria then crawled into my fully-netted bunk on the first deck. Through occasional noise as several guys returned from their own night's adventures, I managed to cover my head and fall to sleep.

Swapping Places

The next morning after a great three-egg omelet, bacon, toast, juice and coffee, I was driven back to Tan San Nhut. I was to meet Lt. Les Bivens in the air terminal when he arrived on a Caribou from Cam Ranh Bay. We would have a short turnover meeting. Then I would fly to CRB, and Les would fly home to Hawaii.

Les had been promoted to Lieutenant but had not yet received official notice. I was given the privilege of pinning on his "railroad tracks" (lieutenant bars). After this informal ceremony, I offered congratulations, and again thanked him for volunteering to take my place on the team, while I stayed in Hawaii for my daughter's birth. I told him I'd never be able to fully show my appreciation.

In his quizzical manner of speaking directly, Les replied, "You've already done it—she was born on my birthday." The coincidence astounded me.

After bidding farewell to Kendra's "birthday twin", I headed for Cam Ranh Bay, eager to reconnect with the team, and Toad, Garth, John, Slan, and Tinker (not knowing the details about Tinker). I didn't anticipate the confrontation that awaited me.

22

What Is Going on Here?
Returning to Standard Operating Procedures

AFTER ARRIVING AT CRB ON 10 FEBRUARY 1971, I SPENT a day getting familiar with Market Time Cove and settling into my "room" in the main Quonset. I was soon ready to go on my first night watch at the OPCON barge. It was now time to apply all my training to operating in a war zone. I was cautiously looking forward to this.

The night-watch crew all piled into the truck for the drive to the ammo pier. Lum, our cook, and I were given seats in the cab, a privilege for women and officers, I guessed. We dropped Lum off at the Cam Ranh Ville gate then drove to the ammo pier. Here we got into a Whaler and motored the short distance out to the OPCON barge.

My assistant watch-stander was GMG-1 Dave Hart. He and I would share the watch for the rest of my tour at Cam Ranh Bay. Officers had night duty on a two on-one off schedule. The enlisted had three on-one off. I don't know who established this watch schedule, but it worked okay for me.

I had known Hart for a year and a half. He had always been very active, dependable, and mechanically skilled (as were all EOD techs). He was never reluctant to accept any assignment, and next to Gordie Sybrant, was probably the most internally-driven man in Short Time. However, his patience level made him better suited for OPCON duties than operating dolphins.

Before I arrived, Hart's watch- standing partner had been Lt. Dave Ussery. I don't recall Ussery ever making an effort to learn how to train a dolphin and I never saw him discussing problems and solutions with dolphin trainers. Each member of the Short Time detachment had a special talent or skill and each contributed significantly to the unit. Ussery's contribution was to be our

Officer-in-Charge and interact with ranking officers of other commands. The diversity of personalities within our unit seemed to work just fine.

This first night, after we off-loaded onto the OPCON barge, I went and sat down at the watch-standers desk and began making entries into the logbook. Hart approached me and said, "Sir, I can do that." I replied, "I know you can Hart, I'll turn the watch over to you later."

At that point I did not know that when Ussery shared the watch with Hart, he had frequently let him run the OPCON by himself. In fact, before I arrived, Hart had run the OPCON by himself almost every night he had duty. It would take more than a few watches together before Hart became comfortable with this new arrangement.

No Free Swimming Allowed

After I had made a few routine entries in the logbook, I walked outside to assist getting the SVSs underway and releasing the dolphins. To my surprise, all three SVSs had maneuvered so that each SVS pen gate matched up with the gate on the dolphin's enclosure.

I turned to someone and asked, "What's going on here?" I was dumbfounded. I just couldn't believe my eyes.

This procedure prevented the dolphins from having an opportunity to swim freely at any time. This was totally new to me, and to our four remaining dolphins. This was no way to treat dolphins that had experienced years of boat-following and free-swimming. This also was not how the system was designed, trained and operated by both the civilians and military trainers for the past three years.

Normally when the SVSs were manned and readied, they departed and drove to their sentry stations, where they made a two-point moor. Once they had adjusted the anchors for the current and were properly aligned, they radioed OPCON. Then an OPCON watch-stander took the Whaler with a pinger and a few fish, then drove a short distance away from the pens. The other watch-stander opened the gate to a dolphin's enclosure so the dolphin could swim out and boat-follow the Whaler. The dolphin boat-followed the

Whaler to an SVS where a trainer called the dolphin into the SVS pen with a pinger.

After two years of operating the Dolphin Swimmer Defense System this way, this is what I had expected to see this evening.

Apparently after Tinker went AWOL on 27 December, Ussery told the trainers to stop the practice of boat-following to duty stations and to transport dolphins everywhere inside the SVS pen. Clark Bowers, our head mammal trainer, had already returned to Hawaii when he learned about the loss of Tinker. Bowers doesn't remember recommending this procedure to Ussery.

Apparently, no one ever challenged his decision. Ussery and Bivens both respected Scronce. However, he was a First Class Petty Officer and they had known him only a few months. Bivens had just ninety days experience with dolphins at that time and was in no position to challenge Ussery. To this day it remains unclear why this procedure was still in place over a month after losing Tinker.

That night, I lay in the OPCON bunk trying to catch a few winks, but my thoughts kept returning to the boat-following problem. I decided that my first move should be to have a private meeting with Bill. He was the most experienced and respected Navy trainer by far, and would have a solution to this problem.

"You Will Be Responsible"

The next morning, after returning to our Quonset from OPCON watch, I sought Bill out. I told him about what I had seen during my OPCON watch, and studied his facial expression. He appeared relieved and said "I totally agree."

He said he could get the dolphins' open-release control back with a little extra daytime training. He was certain the trainers would agree and would work to solve this issue. Bill said they would be willing to spend off-duty hours retraining their dolphins. The trainers believed in the need to return to the original standard operating procedures that allowed for free-swimming.

Armed with this plan along with an ace up my sleeve, I went looking for our unit O-in-C. I found Ussery in a semi-private place near the office area of the main Quonset and outside the earshot of others.

I don't recall how the discussion began, but I clearly remember how it went, and ended. I told him what I had seen at the OPCON barge last night, was not how the system was designed. He told me we had lost one dolphin, and as the O-in-C, he was not going to be responsible for losing another one. I said I was certain that with a little extra training, all the dolphins would perform as they had in the past. He was not convinced, so I decided to pull out my ace.

I looked over and pointed at the office phone. "Okay, if you are not going to change this procedure, I'll call Bill Powell and you can tell him that you have decided not to operate this system as it was designed."

The thought crossed my mind that Ussery might slug me at that point. At least from his penetrating dark eyes and the tension in the air, I could tell he was very agitated. He probably felt that I had unfairly placed him on the horns of a dilemma.

He raised his index finger and shook it at me. "Okay, but if we lose another dolphin you will be held responsible. I will make certain of that!"

"That's a deal," I responded, and quickly excused myself.

No Other Lost Dolphins

I went directly back to Bill and told him we could go back to training boat-following, but I would be held responsible for the next lost dolphin.

"I'm sure we can get this behavior back with a little extra training time," I said.

"Absolutely, and don't worry," said Bill. "We won't lose any animals. The men will be glad to start extra training immediately."

After only a few days of extra training, Bill, Bob Foster and the other trainers had the dolphins all boat-following to the station. During the remaining eleven months of our deployment, we never had a dolphin stray far from a boat. In fact they became so good at boat-following that Hart would take two dolphins at the same time to their SVSs.

John, breaching while boat-following to SVS at Cam Ranh Bay Ammo Pier (the standard procedure). *(Courtesy of Terrence Rioux, 1971.)*

SVS returns to OPCON barge, Cam Ranh Bay ammo pier and cargo ships in the background. Mike Bragget with line and Ted Varnell piloting. *(Author's Photo, 1971.)*

LIFE AT MARKET TIME COVE

Because Project Short Time was officially conducting an Operational Evaluation (OPEVAL) of the Marine Mammal Program's Advanced Marine Biological Systems' (AMBS) program, we had to carefully document all of Garth, John, Slan, and Toad's performances, as well as collect an extensive amount of other information.

As do other military units, our OPCON watch-standers kept a detailed event log. Additionally, after each simulated swimmer attack, men completed forms that recorded the date, time, detection angle, range, and marking performance of each dolphin. We also recorded the weather, moon phase, and tidal conditions every night.

Bill Scronce and Bob Foster maintained these and other logs, documenting each dolphin's behavioral problems, training sessions, and health status. Every day we recorded the amount and type of vitamins and fish eaten by each dolphin. The trainers knew their animals well and were the best judge of their overall health. They notified the Vet Tech (our Corpsman) and Scronce or Foster of anything abnormal. The Vet Tech conducted a close check of any animal the trainer thought might need medical treatment.[1]

A Favorite Watering Hole

At Market Time Cove, the Short Time unit had two Quonset huts, a fish house, a workshop trailer, one boat trailer, one truck, and one jeep. One Quonset was divided into two sections, with four Chiefs living in one side, and nine enlisted men in the other half. The second Quonset served as a kitchen, office, storage area, and sleeping quarters (two cubicles) for the two officers.

After several months, one of the storage areas at the end of the main Quonset was converted into a bar. It became a favorite watering hole for off-duty personnel from other Market Time units. The bar was a mixed blessing, but it generated money for Short Time's "Welfare and Recreation" Fund.

Trainer Jack Brown relaxes at Market Time Cove's two Quonset huts, which held the kitchen, office, officers' quarters (right) and enlisted quarters (left). In the early weeks under monsoon threat, sandbags were added almost every day. *(Author's Photo, 1971.)*

Housekeeper Lum

Before I arrived, the unit had hired a young Vietnamese lady named Lum as our housekeeper. Every morning on our way home from night duty, we drove by the Cam Ranh Ville gate to pick her up. The Vietnamese, who worked on CRB base, stood along a high chain-linked fence that separated the Ville from the military base every morning. Employers would find them and meet them at the gate. After the guards checked the workers photo IDs, they allowed them to pass through the gate. This is how Lum (and later her assistants) were taken to our Quonsets at Market Time. In the late afternoon, on our way to duty at the ammo pier, we dropped her off at the Ville.

By the time I got there, Lum had taken over most of all the cooking duties, although Hart cooked a little. Lum was liked by all, and she was a great asset to this transplanted group of trainers and night watchmen. She cooked well, cleaned our spaces, and washed and ironed our laundry. She was a very good seamstress; she patched tears, replaced buttons, and turned our long pants into shorts.

The Short Time unit's cook and housekeeper, Lum, poses in traditional dress, topped with a cammie hat. *(Courtesy of Terrence Rioux, 1971.)*

Lum in the Short Time kitchen, cracking eggs for an omelet. *(Author's Photo, 1971.)*

A few of us, however, had one small problem with Lum. She insisted on keeping a bottle of fish sauce called *nuoc mam* (aka "cham")[2] under the sink to use with her meals. Chief Dick Pence was the most annoyed by the unmistakable rotten aroma that leaked from the bottle. The odor was so strong and offensive to most of us that Pence forbid her from keeping it in the kitchen.

Scronce and a few of the men learned to tolerate or even like nuoc mam, but only if it was cooked along with rice and pork sausage or beef. Those who "liked" nuoc mam swear that the putrid odor vanished when heated, and it actually added flavor to the meal.

Personally, the only time I could eat it was one night when I was in a Nha Trang restaurant as a guest and had downed my quota of Tiger and "33" beers. I had already eaten several side orders of small dried-up little fish, fried bird heads, and seaweeds. At that point I figured a plate of fried rice with "mystery meat" and a little nuoc mam was not going to kill me, especially if the beers kept coming. I didn't die, but I didn't order seconds.

Soon after arriving at CRB someone told me that Lum was extremely ticklish. I just couldn't resist testing to see just how ticklish she was. So one afternoon, I snuck up behind her while she was at the stove and tickled her under both arms.

Before I knew it, she had grabbed a long kitchen knife near the stove, spun around and was facing me in a crouched position with a stare that clearly said, "don't you dare!" I backed up raised my hands in surrender. Her fierce expression slowly changed into a partial smile, but she did not put down the knife. I looked straight into her eyes and said, "Okay, okay! I'll never do that again! I promise."

Lum's lightning-fast response made me happy I never had to engage in hand-to-hand combat with any of her distant relatives, who might be VC. After this we were friends from then on. I was true to my word and never even thought of tickling her again. I just watched the other guys tease her in good spirits but she fought back at them like a tiger every time.

CRB was turned over to South Vietnamese in May 1972. In April 1975, the NVA took over CRB, and many of us have often wondered what became of Lum after we left. In many towns the NVA harmed (or killed) most of the South Vietnamese who had worked with the Americans.

Local Marine Life

Once comfortable with my regular jobs, I wanted to spend some off duty time diving on the local reefs and checking out the local marine life. The Navy had already sent me many interesting places to dive; Florida Keys, Guantanamo Bay, Cuba, St. Thomas, Virgin Islands, Spanish ports (Barcelona and Genoa), Italian ports (Naples, La Spezia) and Italian islands (Sicily and Sardinia). My Pacific diving had been limited to Oahu, Hawaii and this was not very interesting, except of course the Hanauma Bay Nature Preserve.

The author poses with Dick Pence's off-duty diving results. *(Author's Photo, 1971.)*

MNC Dick Pence was in charge of the unit's Dive Locker and was van excellent diver. Pence wanted to go diving but couldn't find many dive partners. It wasn't long before we linked up.

First we explored the areas just outside the mouth of the bay. It was here that I saw my first sea snake. We saw new and familiar invertebrates. Of all the local marine life, I was most impressed with the large population and diversity of feather stars (aka sea lilies and crinoids). I created a fully functioning aquarium for samples. (After I left, it became a terrarium.)

Animal collecting was limited to relatively small, benign marine animals while I was at CRB. One guy did adopt a dog of questionable pedigree as a mascot but that was our only real animal pet.

Then there was Charlie Wongdock and his cobra and water monitor.

Colorful Characters

Charlie Wongdock was one of the most gregarious and extroverted persons I have ever encountered. He was a Second Class Signalman who had graduated from Navy Dive School and EOD School, and was a qualified EOD technician. He was born in Hawaii; his mother was 100 percent Hawaiian and his father was half Chinese and half Irish. They gave him the first name of Arthur, plus (according to Charlie), "a long Hawaiian middle name including "Kamehameha". How he came to be called Charlie, I don't know.

On my nights off-duty, I tried to get a good night's sleep. If Charlie's night off coincided with mine, this was not good. After a night of partying, he often brought new friends back to our Quonset hut for a final drink or a snack. The kitchen and eating areas were right outside my bedroom (think cubical). He got in the habit of tapping on my door to introduce me as his dai´uy (Vietnamese for lieutenant). I never figured out why.

One summer night in September 1971, Charlie and Ltjg. Chris Frier (who had recently replaced Lt. Les Bivens), were driving the jeep back to Market Time after a fair number of drinks at the CRB Air Force bar. Charlie spotted a snake in the road and yelled, "STOP!" He jumped out and grabbed it behind its head. The snake quickly wrapped itself around Charlie's arm. Chris asked how he was going to release it. Charlie had no idea. Chris (a biologist) suggested Charlie take the snake and visit our walk-in, zero-degree Farenheit fish freezer until the snake relaxed. Then Charlie could place it in my aquarium turned terrarium. The next day they learned the creature was actually a deadly Indo-Chinese cobra (*Naja siamensis*).

Charlie Wongdock and his pet water monitor at Market Time. *(Courtesy of Terrence Rioux, 1972.)*

On another day, as Charlie, Chris, and Gary Shaw were driving the Boston Whaler along the shoreline on their way back from diving, Charlie saw something in the shallows. Without warning, Charlie jumped in and wrestled a six-foot water monitor into the boat. Once on land, Charlie was able to put a leash on the monitor (*Varanus salvator*). He kept it outside the enlisted Quonset hut, fed it kitchen scraps and was always happy to show it off.

Other Diversions

Other off-duty diversions included sailing, water skiing, diving, collecting shells and driving our jeep to the base clubs for drinks at 25 cents each, and watching live Philippine or South Korean bands. On occasion, some men drove the jeep to the outdoor drive-in movies.

Chris Frier and Milo McManus recall thinking how surreal it was watching *Easy Rider* at an outdoor movie as the base was taking incoming rockets.

23

"Lieutenant, What Were You Thinking?" Like a Scene from *Apocalypse Now* (1971)

S EVEN YEARS AFTER I LEFT VIETNAM, I WENT TO SEE the hit film, *Apocalypse Now*. The screenplay, based on Joseph Conrad's 1903 classic novel, *Heart of Darkness*, was written by John Milius and Francis F. Coppola.[1] Milius has said his original intent was to write a satire on the Vietnam War. This may explain why many scenes seemed like exaggerated versions of the war's realities.[2] However, many Vietnam veterans have said some scenes remind them of actual events. One scene came very close to what I experienced one night on OPCON watch at the ammo pier.

Watching the movie, I began reliving a situation that required me to make a split-second, possible life-and-death decision. My choice was different from the movie's version, but unlike the actor, I had to live or die by it.

Capturing Sampans

Each night while the SVS operators were on station, they not only operated the dolphins, but scanned the water using a night-vision Starlight Scope. This is a single-lens, low-light enhancer that allowed you to see quite well at night. If you accidentally looked through it into a light, it totally bleached out the optical for a few seconds.

SVS operators frequently called OPCON on the secure voice radio and requested we check out suspicious sightings. The majority of the time we only found harmless floating objects (styrofoam, plastic materials, logs, etc.) that drifted into the area. Occasionally we encountered a manned sampan.

The sampan was one of three common swimmer sapper delivery methods. The other two were snorkeling, with obvious limitations, and SCUBA, which wasn't readily available to remote sapper platoons. Sampans of all sizes were the most common watercraft in Vietnam. This made them ideal for covert delivery of the swimmer sappers.

Using sampans extended the swimmers' range and the amount of explosives they could deliver. Swimmer sappers could travel freely in sampans dressed as locals, fishermen, or merchants. They could slip over the side of the sampan with their explosive charges and swim, or drift, to the target. (Swimmer sappers often tied a length of rope between each other, then swam toward each side of a ship's anchor chain. After the middle of the rope caught the chain, the swimmers placed their charges against the ship's hull. Once the charges were in place they activated a time-delayed igniter (e.g., chemical pencil) and exited the area by swimming or drifting down current. This was the most common method of attack.)[3]

OPCON always went and checked the object and usually only one of us took the Whaler to investigate. During the four months I stood OPCON duty with Hart, we captured only three or four sampans. The other OPCON watch caught about the same number. In early 1971, all the sampans had been fishermen, and we began to think they must be taking the risk of being captured because this was a good fishing area. But in a war zone you can't be sure.

If the SVS operators could tell the object was a sampan, then two of us would go to inspect and capture it. One would hold a weapon on the fisherman while the other held a spotlight and secured a towline to the sampan while keeping an eye on the fisherman as we towed him to shore. On the way in, we radioed the U.S. Security Police who met us at the pier and took the fisherman into custody for interrogation. They usually just left the sampan on the shore. If the interrogation found nothing unusual, they turned the fisherman (and usually his sampan) over to the Vietnamese Harbor Patrol.

I was told that during the final four months of 1971, the number of captured sampans increased dramatically. In fact, Ltjg. Chris Frier said they took a total of thirty-eight sampans during these months. I learned also that many fishermen never got their sampans back; if they did, they had to pay a high price.

Charlie Wongdock in a captured sampan, the common fishing vessel for swimmer sappers to get close to their targets. *(Courtesy of Terry Rioux, 1971.)*

A Split-Second Decision

This night Dick Pence radioed OPCON that he saw something on the water, north of the pier, about 200 yards from shore. Since most previous sightings had been only plastic bottles and other floating debris, I told Dave Hart he could stay at OPCON and I'd go check this out. I took my CAR-15 and M-79 and drove our Whaler to the area Pence had identified. I had with me a powerful handheld spotlight, radio, pop flares, and two weapons. I believed I was prepared for anything.

As I approached the area, I slowed the boat and panned the water surface with the spotlight. During one sweep the light shined on what looked much like a boat. I held the spotlight on this object, picked up my CAR-15, switched to semi-automatic, and drove slowly towards the boat. This was not easy and required both hands. As I pulled up closer I could tell it was a man in a sampan. I pulled up next to the sampan and held both the spotlight and CAR-15 on him. He was visibly frightened. At first he just stood there looking at me.

At this point I realized I knew very few words in Vietnamese. My vocabulary was limited to *ba muoi ba*, which was "33", the name of a local beer. I also knew *dai wei* for Lieutenant, *didi mau* for hurry up, and *mama san babe san* for mother and baby. It was too bad I hadn't learned how to say *dua tay len* ("put your hands up") and *dung lai* ("stop") or something really useful confronting an enemy!

I panned the sampan and saw a fish net and several fish in the bottom of the boat. The man was either a fisherman or a VC in disguise. He could have already delivered a swimmer to place a charge on a ship.

I continued to search the sampan for weapons or explosives with my spotlight. At some point the fisherman became even more nervous and began speaking loudly and rapidly in Vietnamese. In the middle of all this I heard "Mama san, babe san." Thankful to understand a few words, I was leaning toward believing he was only a fisherman and needed to fish to support his family.

At some point the man suddenly reached down for something in the bottom of his boat. Now I had only milliseconds to make the biggest decision in my life. Was he getting a gun, a grenade, or some other weapon?

At that instant I chose to believe he was only a fisherman, and continued standing with my weapon on him. To my tremendous relief, he came up with a very big fish.

As he held it out towards me with both hands, I thought, *I never want to be in this position again.* After towing the sampan in and turning the fisherman over to shore and U.S. Security Police, I returned to OPCON and got a royal "ass-chewing" from Hart and later from the other men.

But at least I, and the Vietnamese fisherman, lived to tell the tale.

24

Final Fanfare:
Back in Hawaii and Multimillion-Dollar
Fireworks at Cam Ranh Base
(May-August 1971)

F OR TWO YEARS — INCLUDING FOUR MONTHS IN
Vietnam — I had lived and breathed the Marine Mammals Program.
Now my active duty as the U.S. Navy's first Marine Mammal Officer was
coming to an end.

After many bittersweet farewells and more than a few "33s", I said good-bye
to Cam Ranh Bay, and to Garth, John, Slan, and Toad, on 15 May 1970 when
I boarded a Caribou to Saigon. I spent the night at the EOD Villa where I had
stayed upon my arrival in February. The next day I took a commercial charter
flight from Tan San Nhut Air Base to Hawaii, where I reunited with Sharon,
and our now-four-month-old daughter, Kendra. It was indeed a very happy day.

Life was going to be very different now. I had been accepted to pursue a
Master's degree in Zoology at the University of South Florida, with an emphasis
on Marine Invertebrates. But first, I had to be debriefed and pack up our household goods and prepare to leave for Travis Air Force Base, where I would be dis-
charged from Active Duty on 15 June and depart with Sharon and Kendra for
a different kind of tour. Before starting graduate school, Sharon and I had plans
to pick up an MG Midget in England and travel around Europe for three weeks.

Attack by Land on the Ammo Dump

When I left CRB, I was confident our dolphin swimmer defense system
was performing as designed and would detect any swimmer sapper that came

close to the pier. I knew this because I had worked with some of the most dedicated professionals in the Navy: the Short Time men and the Defender Dolphins.

Two months after I left Vietnam, at 0230 on 26 August 1971, land sappers came through the fence on the opposite (ocean) side of the Cam Ranh base firing rockets and tossing satchel charges into ordnance bunkers at the large Tri-Service Munitions Storage Activity (the ammo dump). The attack was the most memorable event of the war for many base personnel.

That night, Les Bivens, Bill Scronce and the newly arrived Officer-in-Charge Chris Frier, were on OPCON duty at the barge, two kilometers south of the dump. (Les had arrived at CRB a day or so after I left Vietnam.) They, and all Short Time trainers, had a clear view of the primary and secondary explosions and watched the huge flames tower above the burning POL tanks.

The Tri-Service Munitions Storage Activity (the ammo dump) burns after being attacked at 0230 on 26 August 1971 by land sappers, who came not by Cam Ranh Bay but from the ocean side. More than 6,000 tons of ordnance, valued at $11 million was destroyed, and the POLs burned for days. Clean up took nine months, with 135 EOD teams rotating from the USAF, Army, Navy and Marines. *(Photo: Public Domain.)*

At that moment they wondered if the event was the beginning of a coordinated large-scale attack. Everyone on duty that night prepared their weapons, and was on high alert. Luckily, nothing occurred at the pier, and the Short Time team — and the dolphins — were secure.

They said the attack was one heck of a fireworks show that night. More than 6,000 tons of ordnance, valued at $11 million, was destroyed by this attack, which was later credited to the NVA 226th Sapper Unit. They watched the explosions that night and saw the POLs burning for several days. The reader may want to experience this event as it happened that night (be forewarned of profanity). [1]

The cleanup was equally massive. Much of the ordnance was scattered over thirty square miles that were either armed, duds or in a hazardous/sensitive state. They also include armed BL-3s and other sensitive, anti-personnel bomblets. Clearance involved modified M48 tanks, M113 APCs and D-8 Bulldozers. The operation required several disposal ranges that were safely away from personnel and facilities. A PACAF photo team took more than 10,000 feet of film. The film was reviewed each night to detect mistakes and to determine if it was necessary to revise render-safe procedures (RSPs). A twenty-minute training film was produced and used at the EOD School, Indian Head, Maryland.

The operation, led by USAF Captain James L. Haynes, took nine months. Haynes had been the Chief, EOD at Headquarters PACAF, Hickam AFB, Hawaii. This was not his first ordnance clean-up operation but definitely his most memorable. He rotated 135 EOD teams from the USAF, Army, Navy and Marines. Several of the Short Time EOD techs volunteered their off-duty hours to help. [2]

The websites of many tri-service units and individuals who were at CRB that night all have a personal story about this massive and very memorable event which was vivid proof that sappers — "Zumwalt's problem" — had been a serious one.

The question was, had a successful deterrent like Project Short Time forced the NVA to attack by land, not by water?

SCRAMBLING FOR REPLACEMENTS

VERY SHORTLY AFTER RETURNING TO HAWAII in May 1971, Les Bivens called me one night on the MARS (Military Affiliate Radio System) a shortwave/phone system. Les had arrived at CRB a day or so after I left. Now he was calling from CRB to say more Navy personnel were needed to relieve those rotating back to Hawaii or out of Project Short Time. I had been afraid this was going to happen.

For the last three months, I had been warning him about the impending shortage of manning levels. Now Les was facing his "aha" moment, and I was two weeks away from leaving active duty. Nevertheless, I was still the senior officer at the NUC Marine Mammal Detachment, because Lt. Ussery and Bivens were in CRB. Ltjg Chris Frier was the only other officer in the Detachment, and he had just arrived in Vietnam to be trained as *my* replacement. It was up to me to take on the uncomfortable job of informing my senior officers of the urgent need for more diver-qualified sailors.

I began by talking to the Project Head, Bill Powell. He directed me to contact the Military Personnel Officer at NUC San Diego and ask for help. The Personnel Officer was not very understanding or helpful because of the very short fuse on this problem. I didn't want to take my problem to the C.O., Captain Charles Bishop. Almost to the day, two years earlier, this same Goforth guy had ripped his pant seams while checking in to his command.

I decided instead to contact his Executive Officer. He asked the obvious, "Why did you wait this long to request additional personnel?" I tried to skate around the answer without blaming anyone for this oversight. Luckily, whatever I said was apparently acceptable. We soon had additional personnel ordered in from other sources.

Years later I learned that they came mostly from Inshore Undersea Warfare Group-ONE (IUWG-1). A few came from the

Navy's fleet divers who had degrees in biology or ocean related experience (for example, TMSN Terrence Rioux). But at the time, my focus was on leaving the active duty Navy and beginning a new endeavor.

I guess having to solve this predicament during my final days balanced out the sacrifice Les made for me so I could be present for my daughter's birth. We remain good friends to this day — at least until he reads this sidebar.

EPILOGUE

Was Project Short Time Successful?

Short Time was definitely successful at preventing swimmer attacks at the Cam Ranh Bay Ammo Pier, but do we know why?

Q. How should success be measured?

A. In 1972, Admiral Zumwalt (the CNO) reportedly sent a SECRET message to the NUC San Diego headquarters that included this statement: "The Naval Undersea Center's Military Detachment (Project Short Time) was the most effective of all my Navy units in Vietnam."

Short Time members were officially awarded both the Navy Unit Commendation and Meritorious Unit Commendation. These awards acknowledged all Navy personnel who served with Project Short Time in Cam Ranh Bay during the period 18 December 1970 to 6 December 1971.

Awards were also given to individual Short Time personnel. Ltjg Chris Frier's personal commendation letter contains wording regarding Short Time's success that highlights an important accomplishment not mentioned in the two unit commendations. That is very relevant to the question of why Short Time was successful.

Ltjg Chris Frier was Short Time's O-in-C from June to December 1971. As such, he received a Navy Commendation Medal and letter that was signed by R.S. Salzer, Rear Admiral, Commander US Naval Forces, Vietnam. A section of it reads:

> While serving as Commander Task Unit 115.9.1, [Project Short Time]
> ...was directly responsible for the protection of ammunition ships and

piers at Cam Ranh Bay. His unit consistently maintained high levels of combat readiness. Through his leadership, his unit was a major deterrent to enemy attack in the Cam Ranh Bay area. He directed the apprehension, search and detention of 76 sampans violating restricted waters.

Q. Why did the VC/NVA swimmer sappers never attack the CRB piers?

A. There are a few approaches to answering this question.

1. Was it the number of swimmers detected, tagged or captured?

No. During the twelve months that Short Time was at CRB, only twice were dolphins released to mark a suspected enemy swimmer. Each time the dolphin (John) returned to the SVS without his nosecup without activating the strobe light. Both times, the nosecup with strobe attached was found the following day, on the shoreline near the pier. Both times, John "fooled" a dolphin (Garth or Slan) in the nearest SVS to also report and confirm a swimmer. Unlike John, they returned immediately, even before John, with their intact nosecups.

2. Was it the absence of high value targets?

No. There were SEALAND and other cargo ships at the pier with ammunition and supplies unloading tons of explosives day and night for all but approximately seven days during the twelve months Short Time was at CRB.

3. Was it because the VC couldn't get close enough to deliver a swimmer?

Probably not. At least seventy-six sampans got within drop-off range of the pier and could easily have delivered swimmers.

4. Was it because the stevedores and dockworkers were local Vietnamese?

Yes, at least a contributing factor. Every morning at pre-dawn and most evenings at dusk, we inadvertently demonstrated the effectiveness of our dolphins to all the Vietnamese dockworkers. Even under low-light conditions they could see our swimmer simulating an attack as he made his way towards a ship. Each and every time, they saw a dolphin swim out of a "funky pontoon boat" (SVS) and mark the swimmer with a strobe light.

This scenario played out time after time for months on end. We knew they were watching because sometimes we heard cheers from the Vietnamese onlookers when the strobe light came on and the dolphin swam back to the SVS.

These dockworkers were screened to work on base and were largely loyal to the Republic of Vietnam and the U.S. military. But we believe that the word got to the local VC Sapper Platoon that this pier was guarded by dolphins and they always found and marked any swimmer that came close to the pier.

5. Was it because of Vietnamese cultural issues?

Possibly. Local folklore may have played a part in the lack of attacks. In Southern and Central Vietnam, fishermen believe in the spirit of the whale ("Sir Fish"), who protects them. A celebration is held during New Year's, and mausoleums containing whale bones are opened for viewing. Dolphins however, signify bad luck. The dolphin is believed to have the soul of a drowned man that was changed into an evil spirit and brings harm to fishermen.[1]

After we realized that the Vietnamese dockworkers may be spreading the word about our animals, some of us joked that we should have brought our killer whale, Ahab, instead of five dolphins and just boat-followed him around the bay. The sight of the trainer tossing five-pound Bonito into his large toothy mouth would certainly be something to tell your friends and neighbors.

Ahab, a Deep Ops killer whale breaching while boat-following in Kaneohe bay. The half-serious thought shared by some of the Short Time personnel was that if we had Ahab with us, that would have been the only deterrent we needed...no need for SVS's or Chase Boats or even dolphins. *(Courtesy of Scott Henderson, 1970.)*

6. Was it because of the Short Time personnel?

Bill Scronce (TD-Chief and Navy's 1st marine mammal trainer) answered that question this way:

"This was the first system of its kind and it worked extremely well. It had a minimum number of highly committed persons, who were properly trained to operate the system. They had no distractions from their mission. They did nothing else but work 3 nights on and 1 night off, shower, eat, and sleep. In addition to night duty, they had specific support jobs during the day and they excelled at these also."

Some of Short Time's "highly trained and skilled personnel", goofing off.
(I asked them to make a dumb-looking pose, and they did far better than I
expected) *(Author's Photo, 1971.)*

The Short Time team that operated in Vietnam pose with Navy Commendation
Medals at NUC HI, 1972. Front Row (L-R) Ltjg. C. Frier, unidentified man, W.
Moore, B. Foster, G. Sybrant; back row (L-R) Lt. Blanton, C. Wongdock, T.
Rioux, D. Walsh, J. Brown, D. Hart, W. Johnson, J. Moore, Lt. L. Bivens. (U.S.
Navy. Used by permission, 1972)

APPENDIX

I. Glossary

ABE: Animal Behavior Enterprises

ADO: Advanced Development Objective

ADP: Advanced Development Plan

AMBS: Advance Marine Biological Systems

Ammi Pontoon: A multi-purpose (ammunition) barge, 28 ft by 90 ft.

AO: Aviation Ordnanceman

AP: Anti-Personnel

ARVN (also NVA and PAVN): Army of the Republic of Vietnam

ATSB: Advanced Tactical Support Base (e.g., Solid Anchor)

AWOL: Absent Without Leave

BPM-2: Soviet limpet mine

BL-3: U.S. cluster bomblet

Breezy Cove: An ATSB at the mouth of the Ong Doc River

C-130: Cargo aircraft

C-141: Large Air Force cargo aircraft

C-4/C-3: Two versions of plastic explosives

CAR-15: Modified M-16 semi-automatic rifle

CINCPACFLT: Commander in Chief Pacific Fleet

CNO: Chief of Naval Operations

CO: Commanding Officer

CONUS: Continental United States

COMNAVFORV: Commander Naval Forces Vietnam

CRB: Cam Ranh Bay

CTF: Commander, Task Force

CTG: Coastal Task Group

CTZ: Coastal Task Zone

CV-2 (and later C-7 Caribou): Troop transport plane

DMZ: Demilitarized Zone

DST: MK-36 Destructor

EOD: Explosive Ordnance Disposal

EODGRULANT: Explosive Ordnance Disposal Group Atlantic

EODGRUPAC: Explosive Ordnance Disposal Group Pacific

EODTRAPAC: Explosive Ordnance Disposal Training Unit Pacific

FMFPAC: Fleet Marine Forces Pacific

GMC: Gunner's mate Chief

GMG: Gunner's mate guns

GQ: General Quarters

GVN: Government of (South) Vietnam

HE: High explosive

HM: Hospitalman

HP: High Pressure

HPC: Harbor Patrol Craft

HSSC: Heavy SEAL Support Craft

IUWG-ONE: Inshore Undersea Warfare Group: One

KMCAS: Kaneohe Marine Corps Air Station

KY-48: Encrypting device for secure communications with PRC radios

LCIL-VNN: Large Infantry Landing Craft

LCM: Landing Craft, Medium

LCPL: Landing Craft, Personnel, Large

LDO: Limited Duty Officer (came from enlisted ranks to officer)

LSSC: Light SEAL Support Craft

LSSL: VNN large landing ship support

M-79: Rifle that fires a single 40 mm AP or HE round or para-flare

MATSB: Mobile Advanced Tactical Support Base (e.g. Sea Float)

MMC: Mineman Chief

MMP: Marine Mammal Program (aka AMBS)

MOP: Marineland of the Pacific

MRF: Mobile Riverine Force

MSA: Munitions Storage Area

MSSC: Medium SEAL Support Craft

NAB: Naval Amphibious Base

NAVMAT: Naval Materiel Command

NMC: Naval Missile Center

NOSC: Naval Ocean Systems Center

NOTS: Naval Ordnance Test Station (China Lake, CA)

NOU: Naval Ordnance Unit

NSA: Naval Support Activity

NUC: Naval Undersea Center

NURDC: Naval Undersea Research and Development Center

NUWC: Naval Undersea Warfare Center

NVA: North Vietnam Army (aka PAVN)

OCS: Officer Candidate School

OinC: Officer-in-Charge

ONR: Office of Naval Research

OPCON: Operations Control

OPEVAL: Operational Evaluation

OPNAV: Office of the Chief of Naval Operations

PAVN: Peoples Army of (North) Vietnam (aka NVA)

PBR: Patrol Boat, River

PCF: Patrol Craft, Fast ("Swift Boat")

PG: Patrol Gunboat

PLAF: People's Liberation Armed Forces

POL: Petroleum/Oil/Lubricants

POP: Pacific Ocean Park (Santa Monica, CA)

PRC 38: Military VHF radio

PX: Post Exchange (base store)

R&D: Research and Development

ROK: Republic of Korea military

RPG: Rocket propelled grenade

SC: Senior Chief

SCAT: Self-Contained Animal Transporter

SCUBA: Self-Contained Underwater Breathing Apparatus

Sapper: Special operations person (urban, land or naval)

Sea Float: A MATSB, 11 Ammi barges anchored in Cua Long River, 25 June 1969 (aka Tran Hung Dao III)

SEAL: Sea-air-land (US Naval special operation personnel)

Seawolf: UH-1B attack helicopter, heavily armed

Skimmer: A 20-foot fiberglass motor boat

Solid Anchor: An ASTB near Sea Float, established September 1970

SONAR: Sound Navigation and Ranging

Song: River in Vietnamese

STROMAC: Acronym from Stone, Rothman, Marcus and Collins, the ONR sponsors for the Marine Mammal Program.

SVS: Sentry Vehicle Station

TAD: Temporary Additional Duty

TECEVAL: Technical Evaluation

TD: Training Device Man

Tet: Vietnamese Lunar New Year (and all birthday celebrations)

Tet Offensive: 31 January 1968 major attack on South Vietnam bases, cities and villages

TEVDET: Test and Evaluation Detachment

TM: Torpedoman's Mate

TS: Top Secret

UDT: Underwater Demolition Team (Naval special operations personnel)

VC: Viet Cong

VNN: Vietnamese Navy (South)

XO: Executive Officer

YLLC: Light Salvage Lift Craft: used by Harbor Clearance Units

II. Who Was Who, When and Where: A Key

This is an extensive, but not comprehensive list of people involved in this historic period of Navy marine mammal research and project development. A good-faith effort was made to avoid errors and be up-to-date.

A. Project STROMAC (Short Time) Sponsors

Bob Stone (OPNAV-OP-987), the head of Navy R & D.

Sam Rothman of NAVMAT.

Stan Marcus of NAVSEA.

Jack Collins, Stone's assistant at OPNAV.

B. Naval Weapons Center, Point Mugu Bioscience Division (1961-Sept 1971)

Jarvis Bastian, Ph.D.: Psychologist/psycholinguist from UC Davis head of dolphin communication study.

D.W. Batteau, Ph.D.: Point Mugu researcher, project head for dolphin communication study using a human to dolphin sound translator.

Clark Bowers: Trainer from Marineland of Pacific (California) and Aquarama, Galveston, Texas; hired by Bill Powell for Bastian's communication study; first Head Trainer for STROMAC at NUC Hawaii Lab; was head of Project Deep Ops.

Martin (Marty) E. Conboy: First military trainer, head of Project Quick Find, NUC Hawaii; expert logistician for transporting animals and equipment.

Deborah (Debbie) A. Duffield, MS, Ph.D.: As a graduate student/trainer, she tamed Tuffy.

William (Bill) E. Evans, Ph.D.: Early Point Mugu graduate student/scientist; with Wally Ross trained first open ocean-released marine mammal; author of *Fifty Years of Flukes and Flippers.*

Bill Gilmartin: Microbiologist, early researcher with veterinarian Dr. John Simpson at Point Mugu, then NUC San Diego and NMFS Hawaii.

John Hall: Zoologist, early Point Mugu trainer of Pacific white-sided dolphin (Pat & Peanuts) for SeaLab III.

Blair Irvine: Biologist and early Point Mugu trainer for Tuffy, Rascal, Rounder for SeaLab III, and Red Eye for swimmer detection proof-of-concept study.

Rock Irvine: Early Point Mugu trainer, now a retired veterinarian.

C. Scott Johnson Ph.D.: Physicist, researcher, shark expert, and conducted first dolphin hearing threshold study.

Thomas G. Lang Ph.D.: Hydrodynamicist from NOTS Pasadena, project head for Notty study and first manager for NOTS Cetacean Research Program.

Steve Leatherwood: Writer, marine mammal ecologist, co-researcher with Bill Evans, author of many marine mammal reports and books.

Don McSheehy: Former Director of Training at St. Petersburg (Florida) Aquatarium; Ridgway hired him to be an early Point Mugu trainer; later became head animal trainer for Short Time at NUC HI; also, he named Slan.

Bill A. Powell: Left the U.S. Foreign Service and was hired by NOTS, China Lake, was sent to Point Mugu to manage/research; became the first Marine Mammal Program manager at NUC Hawaii Lab and NUC San Diego.

Sam H. Ridgway, Ph.D., DVM: First full-time marine mammal veterinarian, early employee at Point Mugu, then NUC San Diego; author of *Dolphin Doctor*, authored and co-authored countless scientific journal articles, Adjunct Professor at UCSD, co-founder and first president of the National Marine Mammal Foundation.

Wally Ross: Early animal trainer at Pacific Ocean Park, NMC-Point Mugu, and Animal Behavior Enterprises; with Bill Evans trained first open ocean-released marine mammal (a California sea lion).

Bill Scronce: First military trainer; retired from Navy and civil service; now works for the National Marine Mammal Foundation.

John Simpson, DVM: Veterinarian, pathologist and animal health officer Point Mugu; assisted Sam Ridgway.

Morris (Mo) J. Wintermantel: An early Pacific Ocean Park and Point Mugu animal trainer, animal capturer, and manager of all animal facilities, water quality and holding tanks.

Forrest Glen (Woody) Wood: Curator at Marineland of Florida, first hired to manage Point Mugu researchers, moved to NUC San Diego; author of *Marine Mammals and Man*.

C. Naval Ordnance Test Station (NOTS)

Bob Bailey: Hired in 1962 by McLean, NOTS TD, to be the first Director of Training at Point Mugu, a trainer and owner of ABE; managed Fitzgerald's Keys facility 1968-69; trained the Navy's first open-ocean released dolphin.

Dan Hightower: Rocket scientist at NOTS; later division head, developed Submersible Vehicles at NUC Hawaii; was the first NUC employee to move to Hawaii (November 1967, provided engineering support for the MMP before Hop Porter arrived.

Bill McLean: Technical Director of NOTS and later NUC; was the creative genius and founder of the Navy's Marine Mammal Research that led to the Advanced Marine Biological Systems Program of today; held 49 patents and also remembered for designing the Sidewinder missile.

Don Moore: Engineer, a department head at NOTS, then head of Ocean Engineering, NUC Hawaii.

Doug Murphy: Designed prototype SVS, the Short Time SVS, nosecup strobe release device; also worked on submersible design and development at NUC Hawaii.

Ralph Penner: Trainer at Marineland of Pacific, first NOTS contract trainer; trained Notty; Head Trainer for Linear Sweep, Stellar sea lion "Roland" and other research animals.

Larry Phillips: Served in US Air Force, hired at NOTS, China Lake as electrician, moved to NUC Hawaii; SVS boat Captain and trainer, co-patent holder for the SCAT, was special project officer, and materiel support officer for Short Time during deployments.

Homer O. ("Hop") Porter: Rocket scientist at NOTS, division head for Engineering Support of Marine Mammal Programs at NUC Hawaii and later headed the AMBS programs at NUC San Diego.

Art Schlosser: Worked for Talkington at NUC San Diego, was division head of Ocean Engineering, and built three Short Time SVSs in only ninety days.

Howard Talkington: Head of Engineering at NOTS, later at NUC San Diego.

D. Naval Undersea R & D Center and Naval Undersea Center (NUC)

Charles Bishop, CAPT: Commanding Officer NUC San Diego (1968-Sept 72).

Betty Box: CAPT Charlie Bishop's Secretary at NUC San Diego.

Thelma Flowers: Dr. McLean's Secretary at NUC San Diego.

George R. Langford CDR: Chief Staff Officer at NUC San Diego (1968-Jan 1971) (reported to have said Tinker left because she didn't want to fight in a war).

E. NUC Hawaii Laboratory- founded late 1967 (officially early 1968)

(First to Arrive — November 1967-January 1968)

Dan Hightower, Bill Powell, Clark Bowers and Don McSheehy. (See above for descriptions.)

(Arrived Later in 1968)

John Allen, DVM: Marine mammal veterinarian at NUC HI.

Ron Beaman: Engineer from NOTS China Lake.

Roger Buescher: Engineer from Pasadena Lab.

Jessie Burke: NUC Hawaii Lab Director from China Lake Air Facility.

Adam Camara: Worked in facilities, NUC Hawaii.

Harry Chalmers: Engineer from NOTS, built and designed parts of SVS, and Quick Find Boat, and much more engineering support.

Norm Estabrook: Engineer from Pasadena Lab.

Evan C. Evan III: Biophysicist from Radiation Lab in San Francisco.

Bob Flood: All-purpose engineer/electrical/engine controls/mechanic.

Lee Greg: Assistant to lab director (hired by Burke).

Candace (Candy) Jacobs, DVM, Capt., Air Force: second female Marine Mammal Vet.

Paul Jones: One of "Bill Steele's marines".

Harold Jording: First to work with Bill Steele at Hawaii Lab.

Rick Kahakina: Trainer.

Brooks Levan: Engineer, machinist from NOTS.

John Lindquist: Machinist from NOTS, ran machine shop at NUC Hawaii.

Pete Makalii: One of "Bill Steele's marines."

Sally Matsuda: Powell's administrative assistant/secretary.

Kelly McSheehy: Purchasing department head and much more.

Doug Murphy: (See above.)

Don Moore: (See above.)

Paul Natchtigal, Ph.D.: Behavioral psychologist from University of Hawaii.

Dick Pearce, Ph.D.: UC Santa Cruz Biochemist, yearly visiting scientist.

Ross Pepper, Ph.D.: Behavioral psychologist (Ethologist); believe retired.

Homer O. (Hop) Porter: (See above.)

Dick Soule: Engineer from Radiation Lab in San Francisco.

J. William (Bill) Steele: Retired Navy EOD lieutenant; moonlighted for Fitzgerald's project in Key West was NUC HI facilities construction boss.

Paul Tam: One of "Bill Steele's marines".

Tom Strickland: Engineer moved from NOTS, Pasadena Lab.

(Other NUC Hawaii Lab Primary Civilian Dolphin Trainers)

John Barnes: Trainer, Bill Steele's brother-in-law; lives in Hawaii.

Clark Bowers: (See above.)

Don McSheehy: (See above.)

Norm Chun: Swimmer, trainer; scientist at NUC Hawaii; retired in Hawaii.

Larry Clark: Trainer who replaced Greenwood as project manager for Sea Search, a precursor of the MK-7 mine location system.

Jim Corey: Head Trainer at St. Petersburg (Florida) Aquatarium; became NUC trainer for Quick Find and other programs; Military Tech. Rep., retired civil service in San Diego, California.

Ralph Hawn: Contract trainer from SeaLife Park; left in summer 1969.

Scott Henderson: Swimmer, trainer for Toad and Deep Ops whales Morgan, Ishmael, and Ahab.

Larry Landis: Ex-Marine; swimmer later handler/trainer for Garth.

Chuck Loving: Trainer for Garth; left in 1969.

Milo McManus: Trainer at Marineland of Pacific, trainer for Slan and Tinker; Tech Rep. for Short Time in Vietnam, retired civil service in Seabeck, WA.

George Peabody: Trainer for Slan; left program in 1968-69.

Brooks Robbins: Named Tinker and her trainer; came from Galveston (Texas) Oceanarium.

Michael Schultz: Ex-Marine; swimmer then trainer for Garth; NOSC/SPAWARs Tech Rep. for MM systems, retired civil service in San Diego.

F. Vietnam Deployment

(Military Personnel First Team, EOD — Arrived Summer-Fall 1969)

John Cirelli: Senior Chief Torpedoman, Admin., OPCON.

Robert (Bob) Foster: Chief Gunner's Mate Guns; Fish Freezers, animals, engines.

Harold (Hal) W. Goforth, Jr., Ltjg.-Lt: Assistant Officer-in-Charge.

Richard (Dick) Pence: Chief Mineman, Dive Locker.

Paul McGraw: Machinist Mate Chief; Quick Find/reassigned in 1970 to EODGRUPAC.

Gordon (Gordie) Sybrant: Chief Torpedoman, Engines, also a Quick Find trainer.

David (Dave) I. Ussery, Lt.-LCDR: Officer-in-Charge.

(Military Personnel First Team, Non-EOD — Arrived 1969-Early 1970)

Mike Bragget: Seaman-3rd Class, Ocean Systems Technician, trained Slan with Pence.

Margaret Monthan: Ensign, niece of Secretary of the Navy, Military Det. administrative assistant.

Art Turnbough: Boatswain's mate 2nd Class; in charge of boats, trainer.

(Second Team. All EOD — Arrived September/October 1970)

Les Bivens, Ltjg.-Lt.: Assistant Officer-in-Charge.

Jack Brown; TM-1-Torpedoman's mate, trained John with Wongdock.

Dave Hart: GMG-1- Gunner's mate, Weapons and OPCON (did not train dolphins at CRB).

Willie Roebuck: AO-1, Aviation Ordnanceman.

Bill Scronce: TD-1 (made Chief) Technical Deviceman, trained all dolphins, original Point Mugu Navy trainer, trained Tuffy for deep dive record.

Ted Varnell: AO-1, Aviation Ordnanceman; trained John.

Dave Walsh: TM-1, Torpedoman's mate, multiple animal trainer.

Charlie Wongdock: SM-2 (later made Chief), Signalman, trained John.

(Third Team — Arrived after February-September 1971)

Chris Frier: Ltjg-Lt., Fleet Diver, was Asst. and then O-in-C at CRB; left Navy after Guam.

Jerry Moore: Chief; from Point Mugu, Fleet Diver (Harbor Clearance).

Terrence Rioux: TMSN (DV) later 3rd class, Torpedoman's mate; trained John in CRB and various dolphins in Guam.

Gary Shaw: EM-1, Electrician's mate, EOD, replacement came to CRB summer 1971.

Metzler: UDT; came in last half of 1971.

(Veterinary Techs)

Bush: HMC, corpsman, animal care, handler.

Harris: HM-1 (SOT) corpsman, animal care, handler.

Walter Moore: HM-2 (SOT) corpsman, replaced Harris.

III. Key Players-Life after Short Time

Admiral E. R. (Bud) Zumwalt: Was COMNAVFORV from September 1968 to July 1970, then became Chief of Naval Operations (CNO) until he retired from that position in July 1974. He published *On Watch: A Memoir* (Quadrangle/New York Times Book Co.) in 1976 and that year ran unsuccessfully for the U.S. Senate from Virginia. He died on 2 January 2000.

Les Bivens: Completed his tour in Cam Ranh Bay in the summer of 1971. He returned to help move Short Time to Apra Harbor, Guam, that December. He stayed with Short Time in Guam and rotated back to the Hawaii Lab where he completed his active duty October 1972. He was immediately hired as a contractor by NUC San Diego for eighteen months, then hired as a civil servant as Bill Powell's administrator. He worked at the Navy's San Diego Lab for twenty-six years. His last job was Marine Bioscience Division Head until he retired in 2000. He and his wife, Junko, live in Pagosa Springs, Colorado, where they enjoy riding and caring for several horses. Les is a Certified Trail Rescuer and searches and assists campers and hunters in the nearby wilderness.

Marty Conboy: TD-1, first military marine mammal trainer, then civil service, Project Quick Find manager, mammal transport expert, worked at the Hawaii Lab until it closed, retired in Hillsborough, Oregon, died 1999.

Bill Evans: Transferred from Point Mugu to NUC San Diego in 2010, then became Director of Hubbs-SeaWorld Research Institute. He became Director of the National Marine Fisheries Service (NMFS) in Washington, DC, and went on to be Dean of Texas Maritime College of Texas A & M. He published *Fifty Years of Flukes and Flippers: A Little History & Personal*

Adventures with Dolphins, Whales & Sea Lions (1958-2007) in 2008, and died in 2010.

Rick Fischer: Left the Navy after his tour at the Key West EOD Detachment. He had a home on Big Pine Key, Florida, and was a tropical fish collector for more than ten years. In 1972, after I (Hal Goforth) had left active duty and worked on a Masters Degree in Marine Zoology at the University of South Florida, I visited with Rick several times. We spent every day diving, spear-fishing, lobstering, and collecting fish. These were the good ol' diving days before the coral reefs were damaged and over-fishing took a toll on all marine life. Today, only the Keys Marine Preserves and Sanctuaries come close to resembling the reefs with the diverse marine life from the 1960-70s. The world has lost over 33% of its natural reefs.

Bob Foster: Worked for the mammal program with the MK-7 mine location system. Retired from the Navy; now lives in West Virginia.

Chris Frier: Left the Navy after Guam duty. He worked with his father on an outfitter ranch in Montana. He took care of 150 head of cattle and horses and took groups fishing and hunting in the Bob Marshall Wilderness. This inspired him to attend Veterinarian School at Washington State University. After graduating, he started a small animal hospital in Camarillo, California, where he still practices. He commutes from a home in Thousand Oaks, and enjoys fly fishing at his summer home in Montana.

Hal Goforth, Jr.: (See About Author and Preface).

Dan Hightower: Worked for many years at the Hawaii Lab with various vessels and submersibles. He later moved to the lab in San Diego and continued ocean engineering research and development. He retired from civil service in 2000 and now lives in Sanger, California.

Bill McLean: His creative genius began the Navy's Marine Mammal research and his early efforts lead to today's Advanced Marine Biological Systems program. After serving as the NOTS Technical Director (TD) from April 1954-1967, he was the TD for the Naval Undersea Center until retiring from civil service in 1974. He died in 1976. On 16 April 2011, his eldest niece Margaret Taylor, christened the launched of a Navy ship named the USNS William McLean (T-AKE-12). (http://www.nassco.com/news-center/galleries/usn-dc/take12-gallery-video.html and *www.youtube.com/watch?v=Khm-vsu6CeM*).

Larry Phillips: Worked at the Hawaii Lab until 1975, then NUC San Diego, and later a few years on Water Side Security for the government in DC. He returned to NUC San Diego and worked for Marine Bioscience Division until retiring from civil service in 1994. In retirement he worked five years as a contractor for SAIC, and a contractor for Science and Technology Inc. in Hawaii for a short time before retiring completely in 2001 in Florence, Oregon.

Hop Porter: Continued design and development research in support of the MMP and some work with submersibles and surface vessels at NUC Hawaii. In 1993, when the lab was closed, he moved to San Diego and provided engineering support for the expanding MMP. When Bill Powell was promoted to Directorate level, Hop took over Bill's job as Head of the Marine Biosciences Division and the MMP. He retired and lives in the Point Loma area of San Diego near the Navy Laboratory.

Bill Powell: Continued as head of the Marine Mammal Program at the Navy Laboratory in Hawaii and moved it to San Diego, where he became one of five Directorates in the lab. He received the Navy Distinguished Civilian Service Award for his leadership in developing biological systems using sea lions and "porpoises" to perform operational missions. In 1987, he became Executive Director at the National Marine Fisheries Service, then in 1988 the Chief of Staff at NOAA. He retired in 1989 and bought a small fixer-upper home in France near Chablis, where he and his wife, Dolores, spent summers for many years. Bill planted a few vineyards and practiced winemaking for a while. Bill and Dolores moved back to San Diego and Bill returned to his long-time passion as a musician, and plays in a Portuguese band that volunteers to entertain at various locations.

Sam Ridgway: Retired from civil service and is an Adjunct Professor Emeritus teaching Comparative Pathology at UCSD and the Senior Scientist for the

Navy Marine Mammal Program. He founded the National Marine Mammal Foundation and served as its first president. In 2009 he received the Marine Mammal Society's Ken Norris Lifetime Achievement Award. He lives in San Diego and remains active in marine mammal research.

Bill Scronce: Made Chief while in Vietnam, and then went to Guam with Short Time. He worked at NUC San Diego with various marine mammal projects for Navy applications. He retired from the Navy and worked as a civil servant until he retired and became a Navy contractor. He lives in San Diego and is semi-retired, working as a Navy contractor, and with Sam Ridgway at the National Marine Mammal Foundation.

Bill Steele: Continued working at Naval Undersea Center, Hawaii, until 1993 when the laboratory (then the Naval Ocean Systems Center) was closed and moved to San Diego. He remained in Hawaii and became a *licensed harbor pilot* for ships, and skippered several ships between the Hawaiian Islands from Oahu. He later moved to Jacksonville, Florida, and became an Unlimited Master Mariner with a First Class Pilot's license from both the U.S. Coast Guard and the State of Florida. He piloted tugboats and ships at various ports (Panama Canal, Pensacola, and the Mayport Naval Base) for many years. He is semi-retired and is a part-time instructor at the Navy Ship Simulator in Jacksonville, Florida.

Gordon (Gordie) Sybrant: Worked with other Navy mammal systems at NUC San Diego until he retired from the Navy. In retirement he owned and operated several businesses (e.g., cross-country auto delivery). Died in 2001.

Dave Ussery: After Vietnam he was assigned an EOD program manager job in the Pentagon. After twenty-five years, he retired from the Navy and worked with several political campaigns. In 1984, he was elected to the Tennessee House of Representatives (67th District) and served five years in this capacity in the General Assembly. In 1989, he was not re-elected and became a registered lobbyist for several years. Retired and lives in Clarksville, Tennessee, with a summer home in Punta Gorda, Florida, where he enjoys sailing his 32 foot boat, *Grace*.

IV. The Animals

Navy Dolphins in Vietnam

Garth: Garth was captured near Marathon Key, 18 March 1968, and initially trained by contract trainers Chuck Loving and George Peabody, and later by Larry Landis and Mike Schultz at NUC Hawaii. She always looked out of the water with her left eye and she was very difficult to train to search from left to right. All the other dolphins generally looked out with their right eye (unless an eye was injured). When project Short Time was born in September 1970, Clark Bowers and I retrained her. Bill Powell wanted for at least one military trainer to know how the series of behaviors had been chained. Garth was a slow learner but reliable once she acquired a behavior. One night in CRB, another of the Project Short Time dolphins, John, reported a swimmer; after he had been sent out, and so did Garth. John had just wanted to go for a short swim. Garth realized John was wrong and came back immediately. When Garth died from an unknown disease in Guam 1973, the necropsy revealed an area of necrosis in only one cerebral hemisphere. This may explain her asymmetrical bias in behaviors.

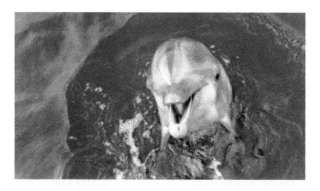

Garth, one of the five original Short Time dolphins taken to Vietnam. She always looked out of the water with her left eye. *(Author's Photo, 1971.)*

John: John was captured off Marathon Key, 1 September 1966. Originally at Point Mugu, he was named by Blair Irvine. In 1968, he was transferred to NUC Hawaii and trained by Don McSheehy. John's swimmer searches took a very long time, and rewards were often withheld. In his early swimmer detection training, he would hit response paddles very hard. McSheehy said this behavior was not easily corrected. In Vietnam, John's trainers were Charlie Wongdock, Ted Varnell, and Terry Rioux. He often pretended to search carefully but didn't actually emit echolocation signals. John also was involved in the only two confirmed positives (swimmer present) reported during the twelve months Short Time guarded the CRB Ammo pier. These two false swimmer reports were separated by several months. Both times the trainer sent him out to mark the swimmer and both times John returned without his nosecup. The next day the nosecup was found intact on the shoreline near the pier. Both events were most likely a trick to allow John to go for a short swim. He was arguably the cleverest of the five Short Time dolphins.

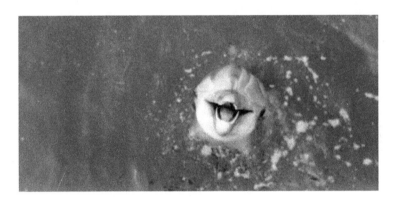

John, one of the five original Short Time dolphins taken to Vietnam. He was arguably the cleverest of the five Short Time dolphins. *(Author's Photo, 1971.)*

Slan: Slan was captured in the Florida Keys, 8 April 1968, and named by Don McSheehy for the main character in a novel about someone who could read minds. Trained by McSheehy in Hawaii and then briefly by a contract trainer, George Peabody, her Short Time trainer was Chief Dick Pence. Pence noted that after being rewarded, she often just held the fish in her mouth. Later, when she performed a poor search and a reward was withheld she'd open her mouth, toss the fish into the air and eat it in view of the trainer. Other times after receiving a reward, she swam around the pen repeatedly tossing the fish into the air and catching it in her mouth. One day she was doing this and the fish landed on the SVS boat's support I-beam above her head. She immediately began swimming rapidly in circles beneath the I-beam (in "frustration"). The majority of civilian and military trainers ranked her as the most consistent and best overall Short Time dolphin. Slan was second only to Toad in hitting force with the marking nosecup. Slan is survived by a daughter (Slooper), a granddaughter (Maya) and two grandsons (Tucker and Phantom).

Slan, one of the five original Short Time dolphins taken to Vietnam. Ranked by many trainers as the best overall Short Time dolphin. *(Author's Photo, 1971.)*

Toad: Toad was captured off Marathon Key, 1 March 1968. She was first trained by Scott Henderson and Milo McManus in Hawaii. Short Time trainers were Ted Varnell and Mike Bragget. She became partially blinded in both eyes after scarring her cornea by moving her head up and down in the transport stretcher during the long flight to CRB. She was definitely the hardest hitting of all Short Time dolphins. Larry Phillips refused to swim against her, and in CRB she broke Chief Jerry Moore's rib when she tagged him. Years later at the San Diego lab, Toad was described by civilian trainers as being the "Auntie" to younger Navy dolphins, and taught them simple behaviors. She had no offspring but made scientific history when she spontaneously lactated and nursed a calf for a neglecting mother. For months, Sam Ridgway left her pen gate open at night, so she could swim around visiting the other dolphins in their pens. Toad worked with the Navy's MK-6 swimmer defense systems until she died in January 2010 at the estimated age of 48 to 50 years. That meant forty-two years of service, well beyond the call of duty. For these reasons I have dedicated this book to her.

Toad, one of the five original Short Time dolphins taken to Vietnam. Despite very poor vision, she served the Navy for 42 years. *(Author's Photo, 1971.)*

Tinker: Captured off Marathon, Key, 9 March 1966, and originally at Point Mugu, then transferred to NUC Hawaii in early 1968. She was named by trainer Brooks Robins after the fairy in Peter Pan. Mike Schultz was her second trainer in Hawaii. Bill Scronce and Milo McManus were her Short Time trainers in CRB when she went AWOL on 27 December 1970, only ten days after arriving in Vietnam. During a practice training session she had detected our swimmer and was released with a nosecup to mark him but shook off the nosecup and swam away. During this training session the Vietnamese Harbor Patrol boats nearby were tossing numerous grenades into the water. All of the Short Time boats went searching for her with recall pingers all day and into the evening. Searching continued for several days but she was never seen again by the U.S. Navy. However, two days later in the evening, a Vietnamese Patrol Boat reported seeing a "dolphin" swimming not far from the ammo pier.

Other Key Navy Dolphins

Buzz: Captured off Gulfport, Mississippi, at the same time (October 1963) as Buzz-Buzz, and spent four months at ABE being trained to wear a harness, and other studies. He was also trained by Clark Bowers for the Jarvis Bastian communication study.

Buzz-Buzz, renamed Pegasus (Peg): Named by Bob Bailey after the sound of her underwater acoustic bridge. She was later named Pegasus (Peg). She was captured off Gulfport, Mississippi, on 6 October 1963 and a week later transported to Animal Behavior Enterprises (ABE). Here she was trained by Bob Bailey until February 1964 when she was moved to Point Mugu. In March, Bob resumed training her to become the Navy's first open-ocean released dolphin which occurred 13 August 1964 at Port Hueneme Harbor, California, and again on 26 August off the Point Mugu Pier.

Cyclops (Cy): An early Point Mugu dolphin named by Rock Irvine because she had a clouded eye. She was trained by Blair Irvine to dive up to 660 feet for SeaLab III (which was cancelled). She also was a Short Time dolphin in Guam.

Dash (aka Maui): Captured off Gulfport, Mississippi, with four other dolphins and used in both T.G. Lang and Dr. D.W. Batteau's early communication studies.

Doris: Trained for T.G. Lang's early study of communication between dolphins. Then she was trained by Clark Bowers for Dr. Jarvis Bastian's communication studies at Point Mugu.

Dot: Captured with Dash from Gulfport, MS and died of pneumonia before she could be trained for T. G. Lang's communication study.

Maui: Maui was captured off Gulfport, Mississippi, in September 1962 along with four other dolphins including Dot and Tuffy. All five dolphins were taken to Pacific Ocean Park (POP) in Santa Monica because Point Mugu facilities were not ready. Dash was transferred from POP to Naval Missile Center, Point Mugu in March of 1963. In 1964, he was trained by Ralph Penner for communication studies by Dr. D. W. Batteau. He was later taken to Hawaii to continue Dr. Batteau's studies at Coconut Island lagoon in Kaneohe Bay. In Hawaii, his name was changed to Maui. After time at U. of Hawaii's Coconut

Maui, an early Navy research dolphin, shown here as NOSC Commander, CAPT Jim Patton delivered the ONR 20-Year Award to Maui, 1984. *(U.S. Navy. Used by permission.)*

Island facility, NUC Hawaii, and Sea Life Park, Hawaii, he was transferred to NUC San Diego in late 1972. Over the years he was employed in a variety of different studies. In a 1970 study with Maui, I experimented with the efficacy of using tactile reinforcement in lieu of fish to train simple behaviors. This involved rubbing Maui's rostrum and area around his blowhole as rewards. However, this made him interested in his girlfriend Puca in the adjacent pen. He became aggressive when not allowed to join Puca and would "jaw pop" at the trainer when he was not allowed to join her. Jim Simmons completed the study after I deployed to CRB and was bitten several times before the study was stopped. The results were not published but it was concluded that sexually mature male dolphins may not be good candidates for tactile reinforcement. Maui and Puca were allowed to spend time together, but they never mated. Maui was presented a 20-year Service Plaque from Chief of Naval Research, RADM J.B. Mooney, 1 August 1984, "for more than 20 years of service beyond the call of duty". Maui was never used in any of the Navy's Marine Mammal Systems. To date, this is the only Navy dolphin to receive an official award.

Notty: A Pacific white-sided dolphin, was purchased in 1960 from Marineland of the Pacific (MOP), Palos Verdes, she was the *first Navy dolphin* and was named after the Naval Ordnance Test Station (NOTS). She was trained by Ralph Penner (the first Navy dolphin trainer contracted from MOP) to study the dolphin's hydrodynamics. Tom G. Lang (NOTS) conducted the study in the Convair Hydrodynamic tow tank in San Diego.

Puca: Originally captured for Dr. Batteau's communication studies for the Navy, she was later transferred to Dr. Lou Herman at the University of Hawaii, Coconut Island, and used for early linguistics studies with Maui. Later they were both returned to NUC Hawaii Lab.

Red Eye: Named by Bill Scronce and Marty Conboy after a drink called Red Eye they experienced at the Red Dog Saloon in Gulfport, Mississippi. Red Eye was captured off Gulfport, MS, June of 1965 and transported to Point Mugu. He became the Navy's third open-ocean released dolphin. In 1966, he was trained by Blair Irvine to detect swimmers in the Point Mugu Lagoon as part of the Navy's first proof of concept study ("Red-1"). Later he, Tuffy and Pegasus were flown to the Navy's Mine Defense Lab (MDL) at Panama City, Florida, to test their range in detecting SCUBA and closed-circuit divers ("Red-2").

Rounder: Trained at Point Mugu by Don McSheehy in 1967, he became the fourth Navy dolphin for open-ocean release. Don also trained him to place packages on drive shafts of sampans in the Mugu Lagoon. Rounder was transferred to Hawaii and trained for Short Time in Guam, December 1972-73, to guard U.S. Navy vessels in Apra Harbor. He liked to forage on wild fish and then eat them in front of his trainer. This was a problem; he died in Guam due possibly from eating toxic wild fish.

Sveny: Was acquired from Steinhatchee, Florida, for an ONR project on hearing at Princeton University. At the end of the project she was transported to Point Mugu and used in a hearing study by Bill Powell, Marty Conboy, and Don McSheehy. She was small but feisty. She was later moved to NUC Hawaii and used in echolocation studies by Dr. Evan Cyfeliog Evan III. One day, several trickster trainers trained her to spit water at a simple hand wave. The next day she drenched Dr. Evans when he innocently waved his hand at her while standing on the edge of her pen.

Tuffy (Tuf Guy): Arrived at Point Mugu from Gulfport, Mississippi, on 19 September 1962, with four other dolphins including Dot and Dash (later called Maui). They were taken to POP because Point Mugu facilities were not yet ready. POP had purchased all the five dolphins, but in exchange

Tuffy, a famous early Navy dolphin (see The Dolphin Doctor by Sam Ridgway). *(U.S. Navy. Used by permission.)*

for the Navy transporting the dolphins to California, POP gave two dolphins to the Navy. They took turns choosing animals. Bailey and Ridgway were new at this and ended up with Dot and Dash. Dot appeared a bit lethargic and later died at POP. In March 1963, when the facilities were completed, Dash was brought to Point Mugu. In May 1964, POP closed its dolphin show, and the Navy was offered Tuffy (1 of the 5 captured in 1962) for $150. He was first named Tuf Guy by Wally Ross, later changed to Tuffy by Forrest G. (Woody) Wood. He was taken to the Point Mugu Bioscience Facility and "tamed" that summer (1964) by a graduate student, Debbie Duffield. Tuffy was the Navy's second open-ocean released dolphin and worked with SeaLab II "aquanauts", in September 1965 off La Jolla, California. Mo, Blair Irvine, and Bill Scronce trained him to dive and locate pingered objects on the bottom. Later in 1969 Scronce trained Tuffy to perform a command dive to 990 feet, setting a record. Tuffy is the dolphin featured in most Navy movies and the book, *The Dolphin Doctor*, 1987, by Sam H. Ridgway, DVM, Ph.D.

Non-Navy Dolphins

Flipper: The famous fictitious dolphin was actually Mitzi and four other dolphins. She belonged to Milton Santini and lived at his Flipper's Sea School at Grassy Key, Florida. She starred in the movie *Flipper*, which was written in 1961 by Ricou Browning and Jack Cowden. The movie was filmed in Nassau by Ivan Tors in 1962 and released in 1963.

(Author's clipping from Orlando Sentinel, 1972.)

Original 'Flipper' Dies At 20

GRASSY KEY (UPI)— Mitzi, the seven-foot dolphin featured as "Flipper" in the original movie eight years ago, has died of a heart attack, it was disclosed Thursday.

Mitzi's owners said the talented dolphin died in their arms on June 25 at the tourist attraction built around her act. Her age was estimated at "20 years-plus."

Mitzi was the first of a number of dolphins to play the Flipper role.

She was netted by Mr. and Mrs. Milton Santini in 1961 and two years later starred in the MGM movie, forerunner of a long-run television series.

Mitzi never was filmed specifically for television, but clips from the movie were frequently used on the TV series in place of other dolphins who appeared in the lead role.

"There wasn't another one like her in the world, and there never will be," said Mrs. Santini. "She seemed to be more anxious to please, a showoff, a real ham."

When Mitzi was first netted, the Santinis were in the business of capturing and selling dolphins. They decided to keep Mitzi in order to have a tame porpoise around to calm other newcomers.

It didn't take long for Mrs. Santini to realize she had something special. Soon after the Santinis

7-FOOT DOLPHIN A REAL HAM
. . . Mitzi first to play role

brought Mitzi back home to the Florida keys, Mrs. Santini discovered "I could pet and play with her."

Pretty soon, I got curious as to what she would do if I got in the pool with her."

"She was frightened at first and it took two hours before she would come up close enough to take the fish I had in my hand," she said.

But Mitzi soon lost her fear of her human companion. Once as Mitzi ap-proached for a handout, Mrs. Santini said, "I grabbed her dorsal fin and away we went."

Mitzi's eagerness to tow humans around her pool landed her the movie role.

Mrs. Santini said Mitzi died in the arms of the Santinis after a night of trying to beach herself in the shallow part of the pool in order to keep her blowhole out of the water and avoid drowning in her weakness.

Keiki: A Pacific Bottlenose dolphin, trained by Dr. Ken Norris at the Oceanic Institute, Oahu became the second open-ocean released dolphin on 28 August 1964. This was only ten days after the Navy's open-ocean release of Buzz-Buzz by trainer Bob Bailey.

Mitzi (aka "Flipper"): Caught off Marathon Key by Milton Santini in 1961 was the first "Flipper", and belonged to the Santini Porpoise School at Grassy Key, Florida. Ricou Browning selected her to play the role of Flipper. He and his son trained Mitzi to perform various surface and underwater behaviors in the presence of multiple visual and acoustic distractions. Mitzi was reported to have died of a heart attack in 1972 at an estimated age of 20 (Orlando Sentinel, 15 July 1972). There is a memorial grave site for her in a garden at the Dolphin Research Center at Grassy Key, Florida.

Nellie: Born 27 February 1953 at Marineland of Florida (then Marine Studios), Nellie is the oldest living Atlantic Bottlenose dolphin born in captivity (now 59 years old).

Dolly: She was initially captured by Santini for Fitzgerald's "secret" project at Fleming Key on a Key West Navy base. When Fitzgerald's program was closed in 1969, she and five other dolphins were being transferred by the Navy to Point Mugu and/or NUC Hawaii. Dolly avoided recapture and "escaped" at Fleming Key. She later "volunteered" at the Asbury's family home on Sugarloaf Key. Some time later she was taken to Sugarloaf Lodge where she lived for years with Sugar (another Santini-collected dolphin). See "Dolphins (The Undersea discoveries of Jacques-Yves Cousteau)" for more about Dolly.

Theresa: Originally collected for the "Navy/CIA" (Fitzgerald), she and other dolphins were transported to pens at Fleming Key, Florida. Theresa apparently escaped and returned to Milton Santini's Flipper's Sea School at Grassy Key. Fitzgerald did not want her back so she became a full-time resident at Grassy Key. She performed and swam with visitors until she died May 2011. She outlived a daughter, Natua, and was survived by a daughter, Santini, and grandsons, Tanner and Reese.

V. Timeline

*Includes key dates not only involving the development of the **Marine Mammal Program and other related Navy projects (in bold)**, but also a selection of political and cultural events that influenced the period.*

1960

+ **NOTS TD Bill McLean purchases Notty; Ralph Penner trains her for hydrodynamic study in General Dynamics tow tank.**

+ **October: Bill Scronce and Marty Conboy begin serving as Technical Device Petty Officers at Point Mugu.**

1961

+ **John Lilly publishes *Man and Dolphin*;** suggests dolphins can do military tasks.

+ Ricou Browning and Jack Cowden write book/screenplay for the hit movie *Flipper*.

+ **December: Notty, the Navy's first dolphin, dies at MOP.**

1962

+ Pete Seeger releases *Turn, Turn, Turn, Where Have All the Flowers Gone, If I Had a Hammer* (Peter, Paul and Mary take these to Top 10 songs).

+ 20 February: John Glenn becomes first man to orbit Earth three times in space.

+ **Summer: Scronce and Conboy assigned to work with the McGinnities, at Naval Missile Center's (NMC) Life Sciences Div.**

+ **July: McLean buys three Pacific white-sided dolphins from fisherman in Santa Monica; all soon die.**

- September: NMC Life Science Div. gets two Atlantic bottlenose dolphins captured off Gulfport, Mississippi.

- October: Sam Ridgway hired as the NMC's Animal Health Officer, making him the first full-time marine mammal veterinarian in the world.

1963

This year marked a turning point, both because the first clashes of the nascent Vietnam war emerged and because American news coverage of Vietnam began to slip towards pessimism.

- Summer: F.G. (Woody) Wood arranges for three Atlantic bottlenose dolphins from Marineland to go to Point Mugu; Ridgway, Scronce, Bailey and Conboy transport them in a Navy cargo plane.

- June: Woody hired by NMC to manage the research group at Point Mugu.

- Movie *Flipper* is released.

- 3 November: Vietnam's nepotistic President Ngo Dinh Diem assassinated during Buddhist uprising.

- 22 *November*, Friday (11:40 CST): President John F. Kennedy assassinated in Dallas.

- Winter: Bill Powell evaluates Point Mugu's management, returns with suggested solutions; McLean assigns him the job of implementing them.

1964

- February: Buzz and Buzz-Buzz, two bottlenose dolphins, transferred from ABE to Point Mugu.

+ March-May: Pacific Ocean Park closes, Tuffy is purchased for $150; trainers Wally Ross and Mo Wintermantel, are hired to work at NMC Point Mugu.

+ Summer: Ridgway hires UCLA graduate student Debbie Duffield as assistant; she tames Tuffy; Wally Ross, and Blair Irvine come on board.

+ August: Evans and Ross train Roxie, the first open-release sea lion.

+ 2-4 August: Tonkin Gulf incidents (USS DDs, Maddox DD, Turner Joy attacked by North Vietnamese patrol boats).

+ 7 August: U.S. Congress passes the Tonkin Gulf Resolution.

+ **13 August: Bob Bailey performs open-ocean release at Port Hueneme after five months of training Buzz-Buzz.**

+ 26 November: Goforth marries Sharon Barrett.

1965

+ Barry McGuire releases *Eve of Destruction*; song became #1 on Top 10.

+ February: VC attack Pleiku, and by June, 50,000 US troops in South Vietnam.

+ 5 May: First public burning of a draft card at UC Berkeley; 19 more burned on 22 May.

+ **July/September: Ross trains Tuffy for SeaLab II. CAPT Bond tells Ridgway he can get $37,000 for him to study ability for dolphins to detect swimmers, and other applications.**

+ **Fall: Ridgeway hires Irvine full-time from SDSU (who worked only summertime before).**

+ December: U.S. troops in Vietnam reach 188,000.

1966

- Spring: Irvine trains Red Eye to detect swimmers/SCUBA and report positive; Powell and Bill Evans study dolphins' echolocation abilities for metal plates (media have field day with wild speculation articles).

- August: Rear Admiral Zumwalt begins work at CNO's Office as Deputy Scientific Advisor to Center for Naval Analysis (to August 1967).

- December: Goforth graduates from University of Florida with BS in Biology.

1967

- 8 February: Goforth joins Navy, goes to OCS at Newport, Rhode Island; graduates in June as Ensign.

- March: Don McSheehy hired from Aquatarium by Sam to train dolphins to attach packs to boats; Rounder becomes the fourth open-ocean released dolphin.

- Spring: Zumwalt requests McLean visit Vietnam and suggest solution to swimmer sapper problem; Powell goes in McLean's place, and reports dolphins may work.

- April: 300,000 demonstrate against war in New York City.

- June: Goforth begins Dive School and EOD Training.

- July: Scronce returns to Point Mugu and becomes Tuffy's trainer.

- September: Pete Seeger sings *Waist Deep in the Big Muddy*.

- November-December: Hightower, Powell move to new Hawaii Lab.

1968

- January: Bowers and McSheehy move to new Hawaii Lab.

- January-February: Tet Offensive in Vietnam surprises U.S., shines media light on war.

- 31 January-26 February: Battle for South Vietnam city of Hue.

- February: Powell gets $1.068M for Project STROMAC and begins developing a dolphin swimmer defense system.

- 28 April: Cua Viet, two swimmer sappers seen by patrol boat but escape.

- 29 April-5 May: Cua Viet, Battle of Dai Do Village, Marines of 2/4 Marine Battalion Landing Team, 3rd Marine Division, suffer casualties but hold off the NVA regulars.

- 28 May: Field sappers blow up six large POL tanks at Cam Ranh Bay base.

- 26-29 August: Democratic National Convention at Chicago.

- September: Vice Admiral Elmo R. (Bud) Zumwalt assigned CONAVFORV.

- October: Killer whales (Ahab and Ishmael) captured and taken to Point Mugu.

- 1 November: Sappers sink Westchester County—to date the Navy's greatest loss with 25 KIA and four MIA.

- 15 November: Mekong Delta sappers sink YLLC-4 (two dead and 13 wounded).

- December: Goforth's tour on CVA-38 carrier ends; he reports to shore duty at Ops Dept. EODGRULANT.

1969

+ **27 January-29 March: Goforth and Pippin TAD to EOD Det. Key West diving for DST fused "mines" being tested before later mining of Haiphong Harbor.**

+ 21 February: Swimmer sappers place limpet mines on LCM-6/8 boats, Cua Viet.

+ 2-21 March: LCM mined two times with no damage; 15 March, railroad bridge blown up, Cua, Viet.

+ **15 April: Goforth interviews with Dr. Collins at Pentagon for a billet with the Secret Project STROMAC.**

+ **30 April: Goforth departs EODGRULANT, joins NUC's Dolphin Swimmer Defense System Tech. Eval., at Key West, Florida.**

+ **9 May- 9 June: NUC Hawaii conducts Tech. Eval. of Swimmer Defense System at Key West.**

+ 6 June: Robert Kennedy assassinated.

+ 25 June: Sea Float established in Cau Lon River.

+ **September: Conboy begins Project Quick Find with seven California sea lions.**

+ **October: First killer whale moved to Hawaii Lab from Point Mugu.**

+ November: More than 500,000 protesters march in DC and 150,000 in San Francisco.

+ November: Richard Nixon becomes president.

+ **December: SEALs attack NUC's Dolphin Swimmer Defense System; project is ordered stopped; Hawaii Lab holds a "wake".**

1970

- January: Military draft changed to lottery based on birthday.

- **January: Second killer whale moved to Hawaii Lab from Point Mugu.**

- February: "Chicago 8" on trial; five convicted but later reversed on appeal.

- February: My Lai Massacre becomes known to the public.

- **21 April: Sea Float had gone nine months without successful attack**; three swimmer sappers were killed carrying enough explosives to sink all the Sea Float barges.

- 4 May: Kent State University shootings by Ohio National Guard, four killed, sixteen wounded.

- **1 July: Admiral Zumwalt becomes CNO.**

- 30 July: VNN Gunship LSSL-HQ-225 anchored 1,000 yards from Sea Float, sunk rapidly by swimmer sapper, which killed 28 Vietnamese.

- **August: Solid Anchor established near old Sea Float** in Cau Lon River.

- 23 August: USS-Gallop PGM-85, sentries saw three swimmer sappers and tossed grenades and shot at all three (two bodies found).

- **September: Short Time born; military detachment expands (Bivens, et. al, arrive).**

- 2 October: NVV LSSL-226 sunk in Co Chien River by sappers who placed mine on anchor chain.

- 6 October: ATSB Breezy Cove in Ong Doc River attacked by swimmer sappers; two PBRs sunk, no survivors.

+ 20 October: Breezy Point Advance Tactical Support Base destroyed, rebuilt upriver with old Sea Float barges.

+ **Late November: Short Time's Equipment Flight arrives in CRB and sets up pens, Quonsets, freezers, trailers, etc. (Bill Steele and his "marines".)**

+ **17-18 December: Short Time's Animal Flight flies to CRB.**

+ 25 December: Milo McManus, Scronce, et. al, tow the 5 defender dolphins in floating pens to OPCON barge at CRB ammo pier.

+ 27 December: During routine training Tinker goes AWOL.

1971

+ 2 January: Goforth's first child born (on Bivens's birthday).

+ **10 February: Goforth arrives CRB, replaces Les Bivens.**

+ **April: Goforth confronts sampan; decides not to shoot what turns out to be a fisherman.**

+ **16 April: Hart helps capture swimmer sapper at Dragon Lake Bridge.**

+ **15 May: Goforth departs CRB returns to NUC Hawaii.**

+ June: Cua Viet Base attacked with seventeen water mines; sinks water taxi and kills thirty civilians.

+ 13 June: *New York Times* publishes the first of the Pentagon Papers.

+ 25 August: 226th NVA land sappers blow up Cam Ranh Bay's Tri-Service Ammo Dump; 6,000 tons of explosives worth $11 million lost; clean-up took nine months.

+ **8 December: Short Time leaves CRB and re-deploys to Guam.**

1972

- April: CRB Naval Air Station and Communications Station turned over to South Vietnamese government.

1973

- **F.G. Wood, Publishes *Marine Mammals and Man* on Navy's "unclassified" history of marine mammal research.**
- April: All U.S. forces leave Cam Ranh Bay and turn it over to South Vietnamese.

1975

- 3 April, North Vietnamese forces capture Cam Ranh Bay.
- 30 April: North Vietnamese Army takes Saigon; North and South become the Socialist Republic of Vietnam.

VI. What Happened to Short Time?

TD Chief Bill Scronce, who worked with the Marine Mammal Systems longer than anyone, has said that the Explosive Ordnance Disposal Commands committed their full support for the Marine Mammal systems during the years they were assigned to them. Scronce was involved with the development and deployment of five Navy Marine Mammal Systems. He served more time in Vietnam than any member of our NUC Military Detachment. After Vietnam, he worked at the San Diego laboratory with the Marine Mammal Program (MMP) until retiring from the military, July 1974. He then worked as a civilian with the MMP in San Diego until he retired in April 1994.

Based on his experiences, he remains convinced that in Vietnam, Project Short Time was manned and operated by the most conscientious and dedicated Navy personnel he ever worked with.

Guam

This changed when Short Time moved to Guam and was assigned to Inshore Undersea Warfare Group-One (IUWG-1). The move to Apra Harbor, Guam, in December 1971, included less-trained and less-experienced personnel, a different work ethic, and different physical and natural environments. In Guam, in stark contrast to Vietnam, there were no obvious enemy threats, and less need to remain vigilant all night.

To make matters worse, three dolphins died there. After Garth died, her necropsy revealed an asymmetrical region of brain necrosis she had for many years. The other two, John and Rounder, were thought to have died from eating toxic wild fish.

All the original Short Time officers who had served in Vietnam had either retired from the Navy, left active duty, or been reassigned. Lt. Chris Frier, the last officer in Vietnam, was soon replaced by a lieutenant (junior grade) from IUWG-1 (non-EOD). This officer was soon relieved from his command for ineffective leadership.

In Guam, the dolphins' behaviors became significantly less reliable, partially due to rutting (breeding drive). This required Chief Scronce to return to overseas duty in Guam to correct the behavioral problems. He had just gotten home from eleven months in Vietnam.

San Diego

Short Time operated in Guam for twelve months. Then it returned to San Diego in 1973 and was assigned to Naval Special Warfare Group-One (NSWG-1). This command included IUWG/Harbor Defense, High Speed Boats, Swimmer Delivery Vehicles and Sea-Air-Land personnel (SEALs). Short Time remained with NSWG-1 from 1973 to 1984, and was renamed the MK-6 (Marine Mammal System). During the 1970s, the MK-6 dolphins continued to operate from the original stationary SVS boats.

Later, the MK-6 became a mobile Swimmer Defense System (the MK-6 Mod-1) where the dolphin swam in front of a rubber boat powered by an outboard. The dolphin searched for a swimmer as the boat patrolled an area. At intervals, the trainer interrogated the dolphin to report presence or absence of a swimmer.

The next development, the MK-6 Mod-2 (Swimmer Interdiction Security System), was a Swimmer Defense System that combined dolphins and sea lions. Like the MK-6 Mod-1, a dolphin searched and reported a diver/swimmer; but a sea lion, using his sensitive hearing and low-light vision, swam and attached a grabber device to the swimmer's leg.

In 1984, the Navy Marine Mammal Systems were returned to the EODGRU-One and assigned to EOD Mobile Unit-Three. The MK-7, Marine Mammal System (a dolphin bottom-mine hunting system) was modified to locate very shallow water mines and was named the MK-8 Marine Mammal System. The MK-8 was assigned to a new command, the Very Shallow Water Detachment. A year later, the command's name was changed to EOD Mobile Unit-One (EODMU-1).

Some of the Marine Mammal Systems were later maintained by SSC Pacific Navy personnel and civilian contractors working for the Navy's Marine Bioscience Division in San Diego.

Were They Ever Deployed Anywhere Else?

Yes, the Marine Mammal Systems have been deployed to the following:

+ In 1987-1988, six dolphins in the MK-6 system patrolled around the Third Fleet Command ship, USS LaSalle, in Manama Harbor, Bahrain.[1]

+ In 1996, during the Republican Convention in San Diego, the MK-6 and MK-7 systems supported the Secret Service with waterside security around the bayfront Convention Center.

+ In February 2003, the MK-6 Mod-2 (Swimmer Interdiction Security System) was sent to the Persian Gulf to guard the Navy's Fifth Fleet/ Central Command assets. They remained until September 2005. This was the longest deployment ever, of a marine mammal system.[2]

+ Beginning on March 24, 2003, a multi-national force including the MK-7 mine hunting dolphins cleared mines from the entrance and surrounding area of Umm Qasr harbor in Iraq. This allowed friendly forces to deliver humanitarian aid (food and supplies).

+ For several weeks in 2003, MK-7 assisted in the clearance of mines from the Khawr Abdullah waterway in Iraq.

+ For many years, a MK-6 Mod-2 Swimmer Interdiction Security System has been operated by SSC Pacific Navy civilians at Kings Bay, Georgia, guarding Trident Submarines.

+ In 2012, a MK-6 Mod-2 Swimmer Interdiction Security System, operated by SSC Pacific Navy civilians, was deployed to Bangor Submarine Base, Washington, to guard Trident Submarines.

The Navy's marine mammal systems (MK-4, MK-7, and MK-8) also have played an integral role in several multi-national exercises (i.e., RIMPAC, MARCOT, Baltic Challenge, Northern Edge, Blue Game and Frontier Sentinel). Here are examples:

> During Frontier Sentinel (June 4-11, 2010) the MK-7 participated in a joint nation exercise in the heavily trafficked Chesapeake Bay. Approximately 2,500 Canadian and U.S. military personnel and government civilian agencies participated in Frontier Sentinel 2010.[3]

> The scenario for Northern Edge 2001 facilitated unit level training, theater engagement, and joint operations in a cold climate. Additionally, the naval exercise emphasized joint and combined port security and harbor defense operations in a friendly host nation. The highlight of the naval exercise, for the second year in a row, was the use of the Navy's MK-6 Mod-2 Swimmer Interdiction Security System to help detect underwater intruders.[4]

> During the 2000s, the Navy's MK-4, 7 and 8, mine-hunting systems participated in four joint exercises in the Baltic Sea (Germany, Denmark, and twice in Norway).

+ In November 2012, it became public knowledge that the Navy plans to phase out the MK-8 mine detection system over the next several years. These dolphins will be replaced by a new high-tech anti-mine system (MK-18 Mod 2) using unmanned underwater vehicles (UUVs). The MK-8 dolphins will still be used for other important Navy mammal systems (e.g., underwater object location/recovery and deep diving tasks).[5]

VII. Countering Falsehoods, Untruths, and Wild Speculations

A. Fitzgerald's Secret Dolphins

James Fitzgerald was an engineer and physicist who held many U.S. patents. When he died 16 January 2006, his obituary contained several statements about his role in the Navy's development of a dolphin swimmer defense system. His obituary was reviewed by someone representing him who said some of the actions and words attributed to him were falsehoods.

Fitzgerald worked at the Naval Research Laboratory in Washington DC for a time, but left in 1964 and founded his own company, Fitzgerald Laboratories (1964-1972). Later in 1986, he founded the Kildare Corporation. In these companies he conducted underwater acoustics research and developed methods to improve the performances of sonar, sonobouys, hydrophones, and related instruments.

He had read Dr. John C. Lilly's ground-breaking book, *Man and Dolphins*, published in 1961, which listed a multitude of military tasks dolphins could perform. On pages 219-220, Lilly writes:

> Cetaceans might be helpful in hunting and retrieving nose cones, satellites, missiles and...things men insist on dropping into the ocean. [They might] hunt for mines, torpedoes, submarines, and other artifacts connected with our naval operations...[and] scout and patrol for submarines and surface ships...[They might be] used around harbors as underwater demolition team operators.... They could do nocturnal harbor work, capture spies let out of submarines or dropped from airplanes... They could attack silently and efficiently and bring back information... They could deliver...warheads and attach them to submarines or surface vessels.[1]

Lilly was the first to provide an extensive list of military tasks that dolphins could perform. However, the first step in having dolphins perform any of these tasks required having open-ocean trained dolphins. This was first accomplished on 13 August 1964 when Robert E. (Bob) Bailey, hired by Naval

Ordnance Test Station/Point Mugu, made history when he performed the first open-ocean release of an Atlantic bottlenose dolphin (Buzz-Buzz) at Port Hueneme, California.

Only ten days later, Ken Norris from SeaLife Park, did the same with a Pacific bottlenose dolphin (Keiki) in Kaneohe Bay, HI. Two weeks before Buzz-Buzz made history, Wally Ross and Bill Evans from Point Mugu had open-ocean released Roxie, a California sea lion off Anacapa Island. These advances with marine mammals occurred at the time Fitzgerald made contact with a government official and contracted to train dolphins in the Florida Keys.

Since Fitzgerald is dead and his work was highly classified, one can't be certain when his work began, or who funded it. Nevertheless, by connecting the dots between facts gathered from interviews and various public documents, I submit the following theory of Fitzgerald's role in Navy dolphin research.

Fleming Key Facility

Fitzgerald said that in 1964 he attended a cocktail party in the Washington DC area which led to meeting a government official interested in training dolphins for military applications. Later it appears he was funded by one of the U.S. alphabet agencies with black research dollars. Fitzgerald spent most of his time in Annapolis, Maryland.

In 1965, Fitzgerald acquired five or six dolphins from Milton Santini, founder of Flipper's Sea School at Grassy Key. (Note: Santini had also captured dolphins for research at Point Mugu and later NUC Hawaii funded by the Office of Naval Research. Fitzgerald's dolphins were first trained at sites other than Key West, most likely at Grassy Key and possibly for a short time in the Bahamas.)

In early January 1966, Fitzgerald had a small facility on Fleming Key at the Key West Naval Annex. His facility was in a secure area, with a small pier, at least five or six dolphin enclosures, two fifty-foot trailers and a large fish freezer. He also had a few small outboard boats and a ninety-foot, wooden Navy Minesweeper (*Mary K*), powered with twin diesel engines, and modified with an in-hull tank to transport dolphins. (However, I learned that the engine noise was so loud they could not use it with dolphins.) They were known to occasionally operate this boat between Key West and Ft. Jefferson.

An aerial view of the secret facility at Fleming Key. *(Courtesy of Bob Bailey, circa 1968.)*

The secret Key West Facility pens and piers. (Courtesy of Bob Bailey, circa 1968.)

Fitzgerald's animals were trained, among other things, to attach pack-ages to objects (boats, piers, etc.) and to detect SCUBA divers and surface swimmers while patrolling. When the dolphins detected a swimmer or SCUBA diver, they hit a response paddle on a buoy or swam circles around the swimmer.

Bob Bailey left the Navy's NOTS/NMC program at Point Mugu in 1965 and took a job at Animal Behavior Enterprises (ABE). In June 1967, Fitzgerald's program manager, Neil Phillips, contracted ABE for a senior ma-rine mammal trainer, to evaluate Fitzgerald's project. ABE sent Bob Bailey to Fleming Key, and after three or four months, he reported his findings to Phillips. Sometime in 1967, Fitzgerald exhibited his dolphins' capabilities to a Navy Admiral, the contract sponsor, and a few Navy researchers. In August 1967, before this demonstration, Powell and Woody at the Navy's Point Mugu Bioscience Facility had already submitted their Advanced Development Plan and Advanced Development Objective for Military Applications of Marine Mammals to ONR, and were waiting for a response. In February 1968, their proposal was funded at $1.068 million, and they immediately began develop-ing a swimmer defense system (SDS) at the new NUC Hawaii Laboratory at KMCAS.

In January 1968, ABE again was contracted by Phillips for Bob Bailey to become the on-site project manager at Fleming Key. Bob Bailey remained in charge of the Fleming Key operation and research as it was winding down in June 1969, and was completely dismantled that October.

Operation Closed Down

In early 1968, Fitzgerald's sponsors of his work in the Keys, cancelled his contract because ONR was now funding the more comprehensive Marine Mammal Program at NUC Hawaii. It can't be confirmed, but Fitzgerald was said to have felt slighted and unhappy with this decision and even threatened to release his dolphins.

For this and other reasons, the Navy quickly arranged for a C-141 flight to transfer his five dolphins from the Fleming Key facility to the Point Mugu Bioscience Facility. The Navy trainers, who conducted this transfer, had great difficulty capturing the last of the five dolphins. Bill Scronce recalled "she was a feisty, female that Fitzgerald had named Dolly." The plane's scheduled take-off was fast approaching so the trainers redoubled their efforts, but Dolly slipped under the crowding net and escaped into Key West Harbor.[3]

Shortly after Dolly's escape at Fleming Key, a dolphin showed up at Sugarloaf Key and became a resident there. It was strongly suspected that this was Dolly.

Fitzgerald's other four dolphins were all transported to the Navy's Point Mugu Bioscience Facility and were never trained for Project Short Time or any Navy swimmer defense system. There is some speculation that Michael Greenwood may have gotten a few of Fitzgerald's dolphins from Point Mugu before he was replaced as project head in 1970.

The five dolphins used for the swimmer defense system (Project Short Time) in Vietnam were all captured by Santini, but they were not Fitzgerald's. Documents show that Tinker and John were captured by Santini in 1966 and 1967 and taken to Point Mugu. They were later moved to NUC Hawaii in February 1968, immediately after the Advanced Marine Biological Systems Program was funded. The other three dolphins (Toad, Garth, and Slan) were captured March and April 1968 by Santini and flown directly to NUC Hawaii. These five dolphins were initially trained by Navy civilian trainers, then by Navy military trainers and deployed to Vietnam on 18 December, 1970.[4]

Penthouse Lawsuit

In November 1977, Fitzgerald filed a libel suit against Penthouse International, Ltd. et al., regarding comments in a June 1977 article, "The Pentagon's Deadly Pets", written by Michael Greenwood.[3]

This was the same Michael Greenwood who worked at Naval Undersea Center Hawaii in 1969 and was released in 1970 for failure to meet project goals. (See Greenwood's Vendetta.)

Fitzgerald's suit lasted eight years, and after appeal was finally decided in favor of Penthouse. Fitzgerald's suit claimed Greenwood had made libelous statements about him in the article. Specifically, it said Fitzgerald had worked with dolphins on a secret dolphin program and when it was canceled, he tried to sell his trained "dolphin torpedoes" or "open-ocean weapon systems" to foreign countries. Fitzgerald tried to subpoena expert government witnesses to testify in his support. The Navy intervened and refused to allow these witnesses to testify on grounds that the government had national security interests at stake and these could not be adequately protected in trial.

Here is the reason the government did not want their personnel to testify. If a witness is questioned about facts A and B, and the witness testifies that fact A is not a military secret, and the government objects to any answer regarding fact B, then by implication one might assume that fact B is a military secret. This form of questioning is frequently used by news reporters and is why those working with dolphins at NUC Hawaii were told to refer any and all inquiries to our Public Affairs Officer.

B. Greenwood's Vendetta

Michael L. Greenwood, who represented himself as having a Ph.D. in Psychology, was hired in 1969 by MMP director Bill Powell to manage a new dolphin project at NUC Hawaii Lab. He was assigned several dolphins, and he reportedly selected a few from Fitzgerald's cancelled program in Key West. He oversaw several experienced trainers, and he hired my wife, Sharon, who had no animal training experience. One of Greenwood's dolphins was blind in one eye and Sharon's task was to attempt to train it to perform basic behaviors (stationing, touching, etc). This dolphin was named #910. Greenwood used numbers instead of names for his dolphins, perhaps to avoid bias or anthropomorphizing by trainers.

Greenwood successfully trained his dolphins to boat-follow for several miles. He had several that could do this, and he enjoyed boat-following them to a dock near his home on Kaneohe Bay so his friends could interact with them. However, Greenwood made little progress toward major project goals, prompting Powell to replace him with Larry Clark as project head. Powell reassigned Greenwood to write an "Operant Conditioning Training

Manual for Marine Mammals". Powell told Greenwood he wanted a complete outline for the manual in thirty days and the first chapter thirty days later.

Instead of fulfilling his assignment, Greenwood performed literature searches and worked on an unauthorized research proposal to reward dolphins by stimulating their brains via electrodes. I occasionally visited other scientists in offices in an old WWII gun battery they shared with Greenwood, and witnessed Greenwood working on this unauthorized research proposal. At the time I did not know, but others told me, that Greenwood was proposing to remotely stimulate pleasure centers in dolphin's brains to reward them (instead of fish) and extend their work periods.

Note: It was a bizarre twist to later hear Greenwood, after he had been "fired", telling the media (and everyone who would listen) that "he left the Navy's Hawaii Lab" because he condemned the Navy's use of implanted electrodes in the brains of dolphins. Just for the record, the Navy never planned research of this type with their marine mammals, nor do I believe it ever will.

When Greenwood failed to meet his deadlines for the training manual, Powell gave him official notice that he would be fired. As a parting gesture, Powell encouraged him to travel briefly to other Navy labs to find a new job. (Greenwood later accused Powell of misusing research funds to pay for his flights to interview at other Navy labs as a bribe for him to leave NUC.)

One of the labs was the Navy Mine Defense Lab (MDL) in Panama City, Florida. Their human resources department reviewed Greenwood's resume and tried to verify his Ph.D. degree in Psychology. They found that he had once been accepted to a doctoral program but never completed the degree requirements.

After his dismissal, Greenwood began talking and writing to media, influencers and special interest groups such as animal rights organizations, colleges, universities, newspapers, magazines, U.S. senators, etc. It would appear that Greenwood was intent on getting revenge by destroying the credibility of the Naval Undersea Center's Marine Mammal Program. His efforts backfired, and ironically, turned out to actually benefit the program.

How Greenwood "Guaranteed" Funding for the Navy's Marine Mammal Program.

At some point, Greenwood realized that all his talking to the media (e.g., *Penthouse, Rose-tinted Menagerie,* etc) was not affecting the Navy's Marine Mammal Program. So he mailed letters to all one hundred U.S. senators, saying he had left his Navy job to expose their unethical treatment and abuse of marine mammals. After several months without a significant response, Greenwood mailed a second round of letters to all the senators. At this point, the Assistant Secretary of the Navy for Research and Development (Robert Frosh) was asked to resolve this issue.

Frosh contacted the Office of Naval Research (ONR) and requested a formal review of NUC's Marine Mammal Program. ONR then asked the Institute for Defense Analysis (IDA) whose job it is to conduct program reviews, to select a committee of experts and review the research at NUC HI. Jesse Orlansky of IDA chaired this select committee, composed of five highly regarded animal behavior experts (such as Ronald J. Schusterman, Stanford University).

This committee visited the Hawaii Lab and conducted interviews and inspections of the MMP for more than a week. The committee members were given complete access to all research documents/files, personnel, animals, facilities, piers, holding pens, medical spaces, fish handling areas, freezers, everything. A few months later, the review committee completed their analysis and submitted a final report to Frosh, ONR and to all one hundred senators.

Their report was full of glowing praise for NUC's high level of care and treatment of their animals, the high quality of holding and medical facilities, qualifications and expertise of the veterinary staff, extensive knowledge and experience of trainers, completeness of all documention, scientific designs and quality of research reports. The IDA committee concluded that NUC Hawaii and its MMP, not only passed their review, but was a model of excellence for marine mammal research and care and husbandry of captive animals. Orlansky's committee report was so complete and impressive that the MMP has enjoyed uninterrupted funding ever since.

Bill Powell and all the Navy Marine Mammal researchers said, "*Thank you, Michael L. Greenwood*, because without the Institute for Defense Analysis 'blue ribbon' committee's review and report, the Navy's MMP would never have been so well-documented by such a highly regarded group of animal research experts."

A Sample of Quotes

From a CBS News *60 Minutes Presents* interview:

> "Michael Greenwood worked with the Pentagon's dolphins for some time, before vowing, 'never again would I sit down out of fear or career interest, when I had something important to say relating to the integrity of research that I was any way involved with.' Soon after, when it was suggested that he train dolphins to retrieve advanced harbor mines from Chinese waters and tag Russian submarines, he balked."[1]

> "In 1977, Michael Greenwood, a former Navy psycho-physiologist, reportedly told a secret U.S. Senate committee hearing that dolphins had been trained to attack swimmers with a device equipped with a long hypodermic needle connected to a carbon dioxide cartridge. When jabbed, the enemy would literally blow up. The Navy denied Greenwood's charges and no hard evidence ever surfaced to support his claim. An anonymous employee explained, 'that CO_2 business all got started with a device that was invented to repel sharks.' It would certainly be a hell of an inefficient way to kill a lot of people. Why not just capture somebody unharmed and interrogate him?"[2]

Penthouse's source for "The Pentagon's Pets" article "was a former CIA employee, Michael Greenwood, who had worked with Fitzgerald in the dolphin program". Greenwood told author Steve Chapple that the CIA once took one of Fitzgerald's dolphins aboard a boat disguised as a rum-runner and released it through a special underwater porthole, where it successfully attached a listening device to the hull of a Soviet nuclear powered submarine. (Note: Greenwood doesn't claim the title of Ph.D. or "Dr." as much now when dealing with the mainstream news media and the Federal Courts. Especially after Greenwood was named a co-defendant in a lengthy libel suit filed by James W. Fitzgerald against *Penthouse*, LTD magazine, et al.[3]

C. Why We Can't Humanely "Free Willy"

The Navy's dolphins are free to swim away every day we open their gates to go to work. They are as dependent on us as dogs are on their masters. Here are a few examples demonstrating how captive dolphins become dependent on their trainers/owners, and how "freeing" them fails.

+ In 1970 at the Hawaii Lab, a Kona storm destroyed our pens in Kaneohe Bay, and all the dolphins were released into the bay. When we came to work the next morning, they were all swimming around the area near their pens, waiting for us to fix their pens so they could return home.

+ In the years before Toad died, Sam Ridgway often left her San Diego pen gate open at night. He did this so that Toad could swim freely about the pen complex and "visit" other dolphins. She always returned to her pen voluntarily.

+ In the early 1980s, I flew to Key West to observe a Navy exercise using MK-6 dolphins (a program that developed after Short Time). Upon arriving, the NUC Technical Representative, Mike Schultz, told me that a dolphin named Dinky had been AWOL for three days. He said the officer-in-charge was afraid to notify authorities or boat launches, fishermen, marinas, and so on. Schultz suggested that since I out-ranked the on-site officer, I should convince him to change his mind and spread the word to the public. The same day he changed the policy, we were notified that there was a dolphin coming up to boaters at American Shoals. A trainer was immediately dispatched in our modified Whaler (with cut-out sides, to transport dolphins) to the reef about five miles from our site. Upon arriving, Dinky came over to the boat and before he could give the hand signal to come onboard, Dinky had already slid into the boat and onto the mat. He noticed that she had been hit by a shark behind her dorsal fin, so he radioed the command. When he arrived, a Vet Tech (corpsman) debride the loose tissue and applied anti-biotic medications. Dinky was left with a scar, and possibly a memory.

+ Navy bottlenose dolphins have reproduced very well in captivity and, if anything, are expanding the population. Because of this, the Navy has not captured a wild dolphin since the summer of 1989. Almost all reputable marine mammal facilities contribute to a well-documented, shared sperm bank and use artificial insemination to maintain genetic vigor. The Navy shares a sperm bank with several larger marine parks. The Navy has several third-generation captive-born dolphins.

Humane Guidelines and Procedures

The Navy has gone to great expense and effort to evaluate possible reintroduction of marine mammals into the wild. They have held two multi-day conferences with both Navy and non-Navy marine mammal experts, professional trainers, and veterinarians. The goal was to identify the most effective procedures for implementing a humane reintroduction program for marine mammals. Releasing captive dolphins into the wild again after being in captivity for more than two years is not possible, according to the consensus.[1]

Here is a sample of their recommendations:

+ These categories of animals should not be considered for release:

   – Old and unhealthy animals.

   – Animals that had been in captivity over two years.

   – Any inbred animals or offspring.

   – Animals born in captivity.

   – Lactating and pregnant females.

+ Assumptions include that the executing agency releasing or training a captive animal for release, must satisfy all legal and regulatory requirements.

+ Selection sites must undergo very thorough study to determine food type, composition and abundance of food and the resident population size, composition, and genetic make-up.

+ Animals acceptable for release must go through a multi-stage training process in an environment as close to the release site as possible. Candidate must exhibit appropriate avoidance of predators, human contacts, boats and machinery.

+ The release site must be the same as that from which the animal was captured.

+ Post-release monitoring must take place, visual assessment of health and medical conditions checked every ten days for at least three months and up to one year, to cover seasonal changes.

This list only scratches the surface of the multitude of requirements and studies needed to humanely release a captive marine mammal. Their conclusion was 1) since most of these captive marine mammals are not threatened or endangered species, and 2) because it is almost impossible to properly prepare and conduct long term monitoring and medical evaluations to the animal after release, at this time release is not an acceptable option. Transferring animals to another facility is currently the better solution for managing excess animals.

Examples of Unsuccessful Releases

The Navy had to rescue or pick up three dolphins in the Keys in 1996. Against recommendations by the Navy, in November 1994, the Dolphin Sanctuary (DS) on Sugarloaf Key was given three Navy dolphins (Luther, Buck and Jake) as part of a program to reduce Navy dolphin population. On 5 June 1995, one of the animal right advocates at DS, Lloyd Good, illegally opened the gates and released all three dolphins. The dolphins left their enclosure but never left the lagoon.[2]

In January 1996, the Sugarloaf facility submitted an application for a permit from National Marine Fisheries Service (NMFS) to release Buck and Luther in Mississippi. Before the permit was granted on 23 May 1996, Ric O'Barry illegally released Buck and Luther near Key West. They were soon seen begging for food from boats in Key West area. On 30 May, a team from NMFS and the Dolphin Research Center (DRC) went to investigate and found Luther. He had lost more than 30 pounds, and had multiple lacerations. Buck was later found near Islamorada 70 miles from Key West. The DRC trainers boat-followed him to Grassy Key where he reluctantly entered an enclosure. He too had lost more than 30 pounds and had lacerations.

At a cost of $120,000, the Navy transported Luther and Buck back to San Diego. The third dolphin, Jake, was so weak when they rescued him, he had to be rehabilitated in the Keys before the Navy could fly him back to San Diego. This cost the Navy an additional $52,000.[3]

And Then There Was Willy

The 1993 movie *Free Willy* was a surprise hit in theaters. The credits included a toll-free phone number for people to call and support the effort to save killer whales from being captured and to stop all commercial whaling. Thus began a 10-year, multi-million-dollar enterprise that ultimately ends up reintroducing "Willy" to the wild — but with an unhappy ending.

Keiko was the animal actor in the movie. A popular but unhealthy attraction for many years in an oceanarium in Mexico City, Keiko was next moved to a facility in Oregon where he thrived for several years. Next he was transported to Iceland then Norway, where after years of captivity he was given pre-release training in a large bay that served as a natural pen. The cost for his care and food was U.S. $500,000 a month.

His caretakers escorted him with their boat into the North Atlantic Ocean where he once lived, to swim with pods of his suspected relatives. These trips ultimately lead to him spending his first week in the wild but when Keiko swam back into his pen, his was stomach empty. On the second attempt, Keiko dove with the wild orcas, but was startled when a pod mate slapped the water with its tail, and he quickly returned to the trainer's boat.

On his next foray, radio tags showed Keiko had visited an area teeming with marine life, filled with herring and blue whiting. This time he spent 45 days in the wild and was 200 miles northeast of the Faroer Islands, 190 miles from the closest part of Norway and 150 miles north of the Shetlands.

On September 1, 2002, Keiko, after spending most of the summer free in the North Atlantic, unexpectedly entered Skålevik Fjord, a small Norwegian harbor, and interacted with members of the public. He had travelled a minimum of 870 miles, about 50-60 miles a day. He was exhausted and remained stationary for 18 hours. Keiko didn't recover from this trip and finally died of pneumonia December 12, 2003, after five years of reintroduction training. The total cost of the effort was an estimated $10-20 million.[4]

D. What Was Printed and What Is the Truth

A great deal of miscommunication has swirled around the development and deployment of Defender Dolphins. Here are some examples.

Claim: "...Three porpoises trained in Kaneohe Bay by the Navy..." ("Porpoise Purpose Remains Mystery," *Honolulu Star-Bulletin*, 25 Dec. 1970).

> *The truth is:* We took five dolphins to Vietnam. One went AWOL the second week we were there and then there were four. (See Chapter 20.)

Claim: "The six porpoises and dozen trainers ...guarded the harbor of the Cam Ranh Bay air base... [An] assortment of different weapons, one resembling a switchblade, were attached to the snouts of the porpoises. ... Sources said there were 'several proven cases' of porpoises killing underwater guerrillas at Cam Ranh Bay." ("Killer Porpoises Leave War", *Tampa Tribune-Times*, 19 March 1972.)

> *The truth is:* We had only four dolphins, not six. We did have twelve to thirteen men, but not all were fully qualified trainers. Most importantly, we did not put weapons on the dolphins' "snouts" (properly called

rostrums). And we did not kill any swimmers the entire twelve months we were in Vietnam.

Claim: "Sources said the porpoises were taken out into the harbor at Cam Ranh Bay in a special boat and set loose. Sailors in the boat used special radio transmitter-receivers to order the porpoises to patrol different areas of the harbor…" ("Porpoises Stand Down From Vietnam Duty", *Orlando Sentinel*, 19 March 1972).

> *The truth is:* The animals were allowed to swim from their pens to a special boat (called a Sentry Vehicle Station) when they went on duty. They were not directed nor ordered to patrol any area of the bay, harbor or shoreline. We definitely didn't use radio transmitter-receivers or anything thing like that to direct our dolphins in Vietnam. We did occasionally use a simple acoustic pinger to recall a dolphin into his holding pen.

Claim: This article claims that the Navy's swimmer defense system (Short Time) that defended the ammo pier actually killed more than sixty Vietnamese swimmers. It goes on to say that two American swimmers (one a merchant seaman) fell overboard in Vietnam and were "impaled" by the Navy's dolphins. All this comes from a person who calls himself a "scientific dissident", a Mr. M. Greenwood. He also claims that after Vietnam, the dolphins were deployed to the Philippines. ("Killer Dolphins?" Steve Chapple (1977, Christian Science Monitor) *Anchorage Daily News*, 9 December 1977).[1]

> *The truth is:* Not a single swimmer or diver (Vietnamese or American) was attacked or killed by dolphins in Vietnam. The truth is that during the twelve months Short Time was at Cam Ranh Bay, no enemy swimmer attempted to attack the pier. After Vietnam, the dolphins were deployed to Guam and not the Philippines, but this is a minor slip compared to sixty dead Vietnamese swimmers and two impaled Americans. (See Epilogue.)

Claim: This article has a drawing titled "Lethal Cone" by Richard Trout that includes a caption saying, "the nosecone is a canister made of Styrofoam, which would contain a spring-loaded mechanism that shoots a .45 caliber bullet." Trout also calls the Navy's "swimmer nullification program a waste of tax dollars..." ("Two Say Navy Plans to Arm Dolphins", *Miami Herald*, 1 May 1990).

> **The truth is:** Richard Trout and Ric O'Barry have been a thorn in the side of the Navy's Marine Mammal Program for decades. They self-promote their animal advocate position in non-peer reviewed media and survive primarily by telling untruths which generate public donations/funding. Then they repeat this cycle. Their drawings and words are misleading and untrue.
>
> The Navy has gone so far as to give them three dolphins (under a Federal Government Plan) to care for and treat humanely. They soon improperly and illegally released two of them (Luther and Buck) into the waters near Key West. They were fully aware that they were required to obtain a scientific research permit from National Marine Fisheries Service (NMFS) to release dolphins into the wild. These dolphins were soon seen begging for food from boaters. With NMFS approval, they were collected and rehabilitated by the Navy. A third dolphin, Jake, still in their "care", was not healthy enough to be transported back to the Navy Lab in San Diego; he was seized by NMFS. In 1999, Richard O'Barry and Lloyd A. Good III were assessed $56,500 for civil penalties for violations of the Marine Mammal Protection Act, by Administrative Law Judge, Peter A. Fitzpatrick. Their actions were publicly criticized and disapproved by the Humane Society of the United States.
>
> There are no gun components, bullets, knives, syringes or gas cylinders associated with the nosecup used by the Navy's dolphins or sea lions. The dolphins' nosecup had a spring-load (pressure-release), detachable cone that contained a waterproof strobe light (nothing more). When the cone was pressed against an object, it released the cone/strobe light which floated near the swimmer. Personnel on watch quickly located

the swimmer using a very fast "chase boat". All efforts were made to capture the swimmers alive for interrogation. (See Chapter 23.) [2]

Claim: The Internet is an absolute gold mine of misinformation regarding the Navy's Marine Mammals. Here a representative site with a title that draws readers, but fails to use facts, and offers only hearsay and speculations: "The U.S. Navy's Deadly MK6 Attack Dolphin Program."[3]

> *The truth is*: It would be futile and a tremendous waste of time and print to systematically address the many claims, speculations, logic, and outright false testimonies (by both military and civilians).

The Navy has extensive information available on the Internet. I recommend readers begin with the official published literature and books by scientists and other Navy employees.[4]

VIII. Resources

A. References

E. R. Zumwalt Jr., *On Watch* (New York: Quadrangle/New York Times Books) 1976.

J. M. Cloninger, *Analysis of Communist Vietnamese Special Operations Forces during the Vietnam War and the Lessons that Can Be Applied to Current and Future U.S. Military Operations*, thesis, Naval Postgraduate School, Monterey, CA (June 2005).

G.A. Cosmas and Lt. Col. T. P. Murphy, USMC, *U.S. Marines in Vietnam: Vietnamization and Redeployment 1970-1971*, Maj. W. R. Melton, USMC and J. Shulimson, eds. (Washington, DC: History and Museums Division, Headquarters, U.S. Marine Corps) 1986.

L.J. Cullen, *Brown Water Admiral: Elmo R. Zumwalt Jr. and United States Naval Forces, Vietnam, 1968-1970*, dissertation, Texas Tech University, Lubbock, TX (1998).

K. Conboy and K. Bowra, *The NVA and Viet Cong* (New York, NY: Osprey Publishing) 1991.

U.S. Naval Forces Vietnam Monthly Historical Summary, Ser: 0789, dtd 22 Sept, 1970, From: COMNAVFORV, Chief of Staff, W.O. McDaniel (Declassified 24 Sept, 1980).

U.S. Embassy (Saigon), *The Impact of the Sapper on the Viet-Nam War*, background paper (October 1969), digitized, University of Michigan (05/25/2006).

E. J. Sterling, M.M. Hurley and Le Duc Mimh, *Vietnam, A Natural History* (New Haven, CT: Yale University Press) 2006.

J. C. Lilly, M.D., *Man and Dolphin* (New York: Doubleday and Co.) 1961.

F. G. Wood, *Marine Mammals and Man: The Navy's Porpoises and Sea Lions* (Washington DC: Robert B. Luce, Inc.) 1973.

S. H. Ridgway, *The Dolphin Doctor* (Dublin, NH: Yankee Publishing) 1987.

S.H. Ridgway, "History of Veterinary Medicine and Marine Mammals: A Personal Perspective," *Aquatic Mammals*, 34(3):471-513, 2008.

S.H. Ridgway, "Being 'There' for Surprises and Delights in Cetacean and Pinniped Biology," The Kenneth S. Norris Lifetime Achievement Award Lecture, 12 October 2009, Quebec City, Canada.

W. B. Fulton, *Riverine Operations (1966-1969)*, U.S. Department of the Army, U.S. Government Printing Office, Washington D.C, 2011.

W. B. Fulton, *Mobile Riverine Forces: America's Mobile Riverine Force Vietnam Vol. II*, (Nashville, TN: Turner Publishing) 1990.

The New Encyclopedia Britannica, Fifteenth Edition, Vol. 12:359-363, 1986.

B. Personal Sources

Several recorded interviews with Bill Powell, Hop Porter, Larry Phillips, Bill Scronce, Bob Bailey, Clark Bowers, Milo McManus, Les Bivens, Blair Irvine, and Chris Frier.

Multiple email, phone and personal interviews with Dan Hightower, Sam Ridgway, John Allen, Dave Ussery, Doug Murphy, Bill Steele, Don McSheehy, Jim Corey, Mike Schultz, Terrence Rioux, Walter Moore, and Linda Erb.

Interviews and emails with Chuck Chaldekas, Liz Babcock, and Tom LaPuzza to verify dates of certain historical events.

Personal Logbook entries of Milo McManus (18 December 1970 to 3 January 1971) and the author (7 October 1968 to 16 May 1971).

C. Selected Online Sources

Brownwater Navy Pages, Ken Hawley, http://www.brownwater-navy.com/, accessed on 10/14/12.

"Pacification and Kien Hoa Province," a chapter of an online book by Major General William B. Fulton, *Vietnam Studies: Riverine Operations 1966-1969* (Washington DC: Dept. of the Army), 1985, accessed at http://www.history.army.mil/books/Vietnam/riverine/chapter9.htm on 10/14/12.

USS Westchester County LST 1167 Association, an online history, accessed at http://www.lst1167.com/history.htm on 10/12/14.

Declassified information on mobile riverine forces in Vietnam, RiverineSailor.com, accessed at http://www.riverinesailor.com/November1968.htm on 10/14/12.

"VC Turn Healing Into...: The Sapper Attack on Cam Ranh Bay from Pacific Stars and Stripes," S. Sgt. Jim White, 11 August 1969, found on EdComer.com from http://25thaviation.org/id301.htm; accessed at http://www.edcomer.com/vnwn-amvet12.html on 10/14/12.

International War Veterans' Poetry Archives, James R. Randall, personal writings, accessed at http://iwvpa.net/randallj/index.php on 10/14/12.

"Commander Arthur R. Lee Recalls a Sapper Attack at Cam Ranh Bay During the Vietnam War," June 12, 2006, accessed at http://www.historynet.com/commander-arthur-r-lee-recalls-a-sapper-attack-at-cam-ranh-bay-during-the-vietnam-war.htm on 10/14/12.

Cam Ranh Bay AB: Stand Off Rockets and Sapper Attack, Bomb Dump Explosion! August 25, 1971, Daniel E. Williams, Vietnam Security Police Association online site; accessed at http://www.vspa.com/crb-williams-bomb-dump-1971.htm on 10/14/12.

"The Anti-War Movement in the United States," Mark Barringer, accessed at http://www.english.illinois.edu/maps/Vietnam/antiwar.html on 10/14/12.

"The May 4 Shootings at Kent State University: The Search for Historical Accuracy," Jerry M. Lewis and Thomas R. Hensley, *The Ohio Council For The Social Studies Review*, Vol. 34, Number 1 (Summer, 1998) PP. 9-21, accessed at http://dept.kent.edu/sociology/lewis/lewihen.htm on 10/14/12.

"Cam Ranh Bay," on Patrol Craft Fast website, Robert B. Shirley, accessed at http://www.pcf45.com/cam_ranh/camranh.html on 10/14/12.

Warboats of America, a website sponsored by Combatant Craft of America, accessed at http://www.warboats.org on 10/14/12.

"James Fitzgerald: Pioneered Military's Use of Dolphins," Joe Holley, January 27, 2006, *Washington Post*, an obituary, accessed at http://www.washingtonpost.com/wp-dyn/content/article/2006/01/26/AR2006012602222.html on 10/14/12.

"Operational Deployment," a private database of dolphin-related information, accessed at; http://www.harmlesslion.com/dolphins/cm_opde.htm on 10/14/12. http://www.washingtonpost.com/wp-dyn/content/article/2006/01/26/AR2006012602222.html

ENDNOTES

Preface

1. Our unit (CTU 115.9.1) later received the Meritorious Unit Commendation, and Navy Unit Citation:

> "For meritorious service while participating in special project development in support of harbor defense in Southeast Asia from 18 Dec 1970 to 6 Dec 1971. During this period, the Naval Undersea Center, Hawaii Laboratory, Military Detachment, deployed, evaluated and developed a new harbor surveillance system in defense against enemy forces in Southeast Asia, and later integrated the system into the Fleet operational forces. The outstanding success of the system attests to the dedication and exceptional professionalism of the officers and men of this unit. Their effectiveness, teamwork, ingenuity and exemplary performance of duty reflected great credit upon themselves and were in keeping with the highest traditions of the United States Naval Service. Signed, *E.R. Zumwalt, Jr.*, Admiral, United States Navy, Chief of Naval Operations."

2. Sam H. Ridgway, *The Dolphin Doctor*, (Dublin, NH: Yankee Publishing) 1987; and Forrest. G. Wood, *Marine Mammals and Man, The Navy's Porpoises and Sea Lions*, (Washington DC: Robert B. Luce, Inc.) 1973.

Introduction

1. L.J. Cullen, *Brown Water Admiral: Elmo R. Zumwalt Jr. and United States Naval Forces, Vietnam, 1968-1970*, dissertation, Texas Tech University, Lubbock, TX (1998).

Riverine Forces included PCFs (Patrol Craft Fast, also known as Swift Boats), PBRs (Patrol Boat, River), (PGs) patrol gunboats, (ATCs) armored troop carriers, SEAL support craft, harbor patrol boats, plus Sampans and Vietnamese Navy (VNN) junks known as Yabutas.

2. James M. Cloninger, *Analysis of Communist Vietnamese Special Operations Forces during the Vietnam War and the Lessons that Can Be Applied to Current and Future U.S. Military Operations*, thesis, Naval Postgraduate School, Monterey, CA (June 2005), 81.

3. U.S. Embassy (Saigon), *The Impact of the Sapper on the Viet-Nam War*, background paper (October 1969), digitized, University of Michigan (05/25/2006), p. 17.

4. Elmo R. Zumwalt Jr., *On Watch* (New York: Quadrangle/New York Times Books) 1976.

5. U.S. Embassy, *Sapper.*

6. Ken Conboy and Ken Bowra, *The NVA and Viet Cong* (New York, NY: Osprey Publishing) 1991, 64.

7. U.S. Embassy, *Sapper.*

8. *Ibid.*

9. Conboy, *NVA and Viet Cong*; Annex C, to III MAF PERINTREP, dated 12/1969; http://brownwater-navy; *U.S. Naval Forces Vietnam Monthly Historical Summary*, Ser: 0789, dtd 22 Sept, 1970, COMNAVFORV, Chief of Staff, W.O. McDaniel (Declassified 24 Sept, 1980).

10. Drawn from multiple sources: Annex C, to III MAF PERINTREP; Embassy, Sapper; brownwater-navy.com; Conboy, *NVA*; Historical Summary, COMNAVFORV; http://www.amtrac.org/1atbn/Battles/BattleForDongHa.asp; http://www.vva951.org/woody-battle-dai-do.htm.

11. "Reflections On My Small Part in the Battle of Dai Do Village Republic of South Vietnam April 20-May 4, 1968," Herman W. Hughes, VVA Chapter 951 website, accessed at http://www.vva951.org/woody-battle-dai-do.htm on 10/16/12; "Battle for Dong Ha," excerpted from *Semper Fi Vietnam, from DaNang to the DMZ Marine Corps Campaigns, 1965-1975*, Edward F. Murphy, AMTRAC.org, accessed at http://www.amtrac.org/1atbn/Battles/BattleForDongHa.asp on 10/16/12.

12. Annex C, to III MAF PERINTREP.

13. *Ibid.*

14. *Ibid.*

15. Historical Summary, COMNAVFORV.

16. "HISTORY OF SEAFLOAT AND SOLID ANCHOR," Brownwater Navy Pages, Ken Hawley, http://www.brownwater-navy.com/, accessed on 10/14/12.

17. References used as sources for information about Mobile Riverine Forces and Sea Float attacks: http://brownwater-navy.com/Vietnam/Seaflt02.htm; http://brownwater-navy.com/gustbook/Gbook2200.htm; http://wwww.Wikipedia.org/wiki/USS_Askari (arl-30); www.history.army.mil/books/vietnam/riverine/chapter9.htm; http://www.lst1167.com/home.htm:USS Westchester County, LST 1167 Association; http://www.history.army.mil/books/vietnam/riverine/chapter9.html; http://www.riverineswailor.com/November1998.htm; http:// brownwater-navy.com/gustbook/Gbook2200.htm; Cullen, Brown Water Admiral; http://www.mrfa.org/bases34.htm; http://www.scribd.com/doc/89719452/U-S-Naval-Forces-Vietnam-Monthly-Historical-Summary-Oct-1970.

18. http://www.wikipedia.org/wiki/USS_Askari_(arl-30); http://www.lst1167.com; www.history.army.mil/books/vietnam/riverine/chapter9.htm.

19. http://www.riverineswailor.com/November1998.htm.

20. Brownwater Navy Pages.

21. Brownwater Navy Pages, guestbook/Gbook2200; and Cullen, *Brown Water*.

22. Brownwater Navy Pages.

23. *Ibid.*

24. "U.S. Naval Riverine Operational Base Song Ong Doc (1970)," Mobile Riverine Force Association, accessed at http://www.mrfa.org/bases34.htm on 10/16/12; "Naval Forces Vietnam Monthly Historical Summary for Oct. 1970," accessed at http://www.scribd.com/doc/89719452/U-S-Naval-Forces-Vietnam-Monthly-Historical-Summary-Oct-1970 on 10/16/12.

25. *Ibid.*

26. The following are sources about Cam Ranh Bay attacks: http://www.edcom-er/VNWNAMVET12.html (S. Sgt. Jim White, Pacific Stars and Stripes, Staff Correspondent, 630th Military Police website; http://iwvpa.net/randallj/vietnam_.php © March 2004, James R. Randall; http://www.historynet.com/commander-ar-thur-r-recalls-a-sapper; http:// www.vspa.com/crb-williams-bomb-dump-1971.htm (Daniel E.Williams, Capt., USAF 483rd Security Police Squadron, K-9); https://www.630thmilitarypolicecompany-rvn.org/History.html (630th Military Police Company, Republic of Vietnam, Unit History Vietnam (1965-1972).

27. Bill Scronce recalls that there were only about seven days in the twelve months the dolphin system was there that there were no ships moored to the ammo pier.

Chapter 1

1. For clarification purposes, "porpoise" is not the correct taxonomic term for the species of cetaceans we trained and operated. These were all Atlantic bottlenose dolphins that are in the taxonomic family *Delphinidae*. That's why I prefer to use the term dolphin. Porpoises are in the family *Phocoenidae*. You may find that some persons from the East Coast of the United States use porpoise exclusively because they eat a fish called a dolphin, which is the same fish as Mahi Mahi.

2. For a more detailed account, see *Marine Mammals and Man*, by F.G. Wood (Washington DC: Robert Luce, Inc.)1973.

Chapter 2

1. John C. Lilly, M.D., *Man and Dolphin* (New York: Doubleday and Co.) 1961.

2. http://www.clickersolutions.com/interviews/bailey.htm.

Chapter 2 Sidebar

1. Jack Cowden told me how and when he and Ricou wrote the book/screenplay for *Flipper*. Jack said one Friday Ricou came by and picked him up at his home. Jack asked where they were going. Ricou told him, "We're going to spend the weekend at Lake Weir and write a book." On the way, they stopped at a grocery store and picked up a supply of food and beverages. They spent the weekend "at the Lake" writing, and the rest is history.

2. For Flipper's theme song, visit http://www.tagate.com/dolphins_resource_center/flipper/flipper_song.shtml.

3. A small irony. I was on the swimming team with Gail Cowden (daughter of Jack Cowden) and had dated her during the time the Flipper story was being developed into a movie. Gail's mother worked at the Municipal Pool where I lifeguarded and asked if I would be interested in doubling for the boy actor (Luke Halpin) in swimming scenes. I said yes (of course), but they used Ricou's son, Ricou Jr., so I missed out on my first chance to work with dolphins (and be in a movie).

Chapter 3

1. This may have been from the same funding source that supported James Fitzgerald's dolphin work in the Florida Keys. The onsite Navy manager in Key West was from the Navy Mine Defense Lab in Panama City. See Appendix VI-A ("Fitzgerald's Secret Dolphins").

2. *The Underseer* No. 23, 26 May, 1967, USN Mine Defense Laboratory, Panama City.

Chapter 6

1. These were years of transitions. In 1967, NOTS China Lake became the Naval Weapons Center and continued in business. The Navy Electronics Laboratory (NEL) in San Diego, became the Naval Command Control and Communications Laboratory Center for less than a year, then it became the Naval Electronics Laboratory Center (NELC). The Pasadena annex of NOTS became the headquarters of the new Naval Undersea Warfare Center (NUWC), along with the Underwater Technology Department of NEL in San Diego, as part of its organization, immediately in 1967. In 1968, the NUWC headquarters was moved from Pasadena (which then became the Pasadena Lab) to San Diego. Also in 1968, the NUC Hawaii Laboratory was opened and operated out of a renovated airplane hangar (#102). In

1968, some of the marine mammal research was moved from the Naval Missile Center at Point Mugu to NUWC San Diego. McLean retained his office in China Lake initially and later moved to San Diego. In 1969, NUWC was renamed Naval Undersea Research and Development Center (NURDC). NURDC as an acronym didn't last long and was quickly replaced in 1970 with Naval Undersea Center (NUC).

Chapter 10

1. Donald P. De Sylva, *The Life History of the Great Barracuda* (Institute of Marine Science, Univ. of Miami) 1963.

Chapter 15

1. Marty E. Conboy, *Project Quick Find: A Marine Mammal System for Object Recovery*, NUC TP 268, December 1971.

2. Clark Bowers and Scott Henderson, *Project Deep Ops: Deep object recovery with pilot and killer whales*, NUC TP 306, 1972.

Chapter 16 Sidebar

1. Because the Army did not win the championship, they created (*de novo*) a second "Championship Award" for the best Army team.

2. Mary and her boyfriend, Tom Stone, ended up getting married.

Chapter 19 Sidebar

1. Uniformed Code of Military Justice, Article 113, states, "Any sentinel or look-out who is found drunk or sleeping upon his post, or leaves it before he is regularly relieved, shall be punished, if the offense is committed in time of war, by death or such other punishment as a court-martial may direct, but if the offense is committed at any other time, by such punishment other than death as a court-martial may direct."

Chapter 22 Sidebar

1. I learned from a SEAL Officer, who was a marine mammal trainer, that these classified records and logbooks were destroyed in the early 1980s, against his recommendation.

2. For the unenlightened reader, here is a description of how it is made:

> Some fish sauces (extracts) are fermented from raw fish, others from dried fish; and some from only a single species, others from whatever comes up in the fish net,

including shellfish. Some is made from whole fish, others from just the blood or viscera. Some fish sauces contain only fish and salt, others add herbs and spices. Fish sauce that has been only briefly fermented has a pronounced fishy taste, while extended fermentation reduces this and gives the product a nuttier, cheesier flavor. (From [http://en.wikipedia.org/wiki/Fish_sauce).

Chapter 23

1. "Apocalypse Now (1979) Did You Know?" Internet Movie Database, accessed at http://www.imdb.com/title/tt0078788/trivia on 10/16/12.

2. "Screenwriter John Milius on Apocalypse Now," a video interview of John Milius by Richard Stayton, uploaded on Oct 16, 2006, accessed at http://www.youtube.com/watch?v=5v-G_c4f9RM on 10/16/12.

3. J.M. Cloninger, Jr., Naval Post Graduate School, Thesis (2005).

Chapter 24

1. "Ammo dump explosion at a Base," Uploaded by James Barrette on Jul 18, 2008, accessed at http://www.youtube.com/watch?v=1H_jtojTq98 ib 10/16/12.

2. Homepages.rootsweb.ancestry.com/~ocs/bios/Haynes.html.

Epilogue

1. E. J. Sterling, M.M. Hurley and Le Duc Mimh, *Vietnam, A Natural History* (New Haven, CT: Yale University Press) 2006.

Appendix VI

1. "Use of Dolphins & Sea Lions in Warfare -- A collection of related articles," collected on Mongabay.com, accessed at http://www.mongabay.com/external/dolphins_warfare.htm on 10/14/12.

2. "Stealthy sea lions enlisted for Persian Gulf guard duty," David Hasemyer, *The San Diego Union-Tribune*, 18 Feb. 2003.

3. "Navy Marine Mammal Program Excels during Frontier Sentinel 2010," Story Number: NNS100618-04, Release Date: 6/18/2010, Navy News Service, accessed at http://www.navy.mil/submit/display.asp?story_id=53979 on 10/14/12.

4. "Exercise Northern Edge," unsigned article, Wikipedia, accessed at http://en.wikipedia.org/wiki/Exercise_Northern_Edge on 10/14/12; U.S. Air Force Fact Sheet, "Northern

Edge History," unsigned, 30 October 2007, accessed at http://www.jber.af.mil/library/fact-sheets/factsheet_print.asp?fsID=10444&page=1 on 10/14/12; "Putting Sea Mammals to Work: Dolphins Help Coalition Forces in Iraq," Nicole Kreger, Journal of Mine Action online, Issue 7.2, August 2003, accessed at http://maic.jmu.edu/journal/7.2/features/kreger/kreger.htm on 10/14/12.

5. "Robots replace costly U.S. Navy mine-clearance dolphins," Sharon Weinberger, BBC.com, Nov. 8, 2012, accessed 11/15/12 at http://www.bbc.com/future/story/20121108-final-dive-for-us-navy-dolphins; and "Navy mine-detecting dolphins to retire by 2017," Jacqueline Klimas, Nov, 23, 2012 NavyTimes.com, accessed 11/25/12 at http://www.navytimes.com/news/2012/11/navy-dolphins-mine-detectors-retirement-robots-112312w/."

Appendix VII. A.

1. John C. Lilly, M.D., *Man and Dolphin* (New York: Doubleday and Co.) 1961.

2. The following are a selection of the sources used: http://globedivers.org/2011/05/21/rip-theresa-the-rebel-dolphin-from-the-us-navy-is-dead/.

3. http://ftp.resource.org/courts.gov/c/F2/776.F2d.1236.84-1035.html; "The Pentagon's Deadly Pets" - http://www.harmlesslion.com/dolphins/cm_pent.htm; "Operational Deployment" - http://www.harmlesslion.com/dolphins/cm_opde.htm; "James Fitzgerald: Pioneered Military's Use of Dolphins," Joe Holley, January 27, 2006, Washington Post, an obituary, accessed at http://www.washingtonpost.com/wp-dyn/content/article/2006/01/26/AR2006012602222.html on 10/14/12.

4. Personal and phone interviews and emails, April-August 2012, Bill Steele, U.S. Navy EOD, LT (retired), O-in-C at EOD Det. Key West 1965-67, NUC Hawaii employee 1968-1976; recorded multiple personal interviews, multiple times 2007-2012- Bill Scronce, first military dolphin trainer, U.S. Navy Technical Device Chief (retired) and NUC San Diego employee (1980-present); personal interview, August 15, 2012, Linda Erb, Vice President of Animal Care and Training, Dolphin Research Center, Grassy Key, Florida; recorded Personal Interviews, phone conversations and emails, Sept-Oct 2012, Bob Bailey, first Navy trainer to open-ocean release a dolphin, owner of Animal Behavior Enterprises, Hot Springs, Arkansas.

Appendix VII. B.

1. "Funny '73 report on the US Navy's dolphins," *60 Minutes Overtime* online, staff, accessed at http://www.cbsnews.com/8301-504803_162-57363208-10391709/funny-73-report-on-the-us-navys-dolphins/ on 10/14/12; also "Military Dolphins: James Bonds of the Sea," Brian Dunning, Skeptoid #260, May 31, 2011, accessed at http://skeptoid.com/episodes/4260 on 10/14/12.

2. *skeptoid.com/episodes/4260; and* "Operational Deployment," a private database of dolphin-related information, accessed at http://www.harmlesslion.com/dolphins/cm_opde.htm on 10/14/12.

3. *skeptoid.com/episodes/4260; see also FITZGERALD v. PENTHOUSE INTL., October 22, 1981, FindACase, accessed at http://md.findacase.com/research/wfrmDocViewer.aspx/xq/fac.19811022_0000078.DMD.htm/qx on 10/14/12.*

Appendix VII. C.

1. "Reintroduction to the Wild as an Option for Managing Navy Marine Mammals," R.L Brill and W.A. Friedl, *NRaD Technical Report 1549*, October 1993.

2. "2 Dolphins, Underweight and Ill, Returned to Navy," Karen Kucher, *San Diego Union-Tribune*, June 14, 1996.

3. "Activists Charged In Sugarloaf Dolphin Release," 1/14/98, NOAA new release, accessed at: http://www.publicaffairs.noaa.gov/pr98/jan98/noaa98-r103.html; http://rosmarus.com/Releases/Rel_2.htm.

4. Compiled from sources: "Free Willy? Sounds nice, but it would just add to tragedy," Mike Thomas, *Orlando Sentinel* online, February 28, 2010, accessed at http://articles.orlandosentinel.com/2010-02-28/news/os-shamu-seaworld-release-mike-thomas-02220100227_1_captive-orcas-wild-whale; "Keiko," J.D. van der Toorn, December 31, 2003, accessed at http://rosmarus.com/Releases/Keiko.htm#Keiko; and "December 12, 2003: Keiko's life has ended," Howard Garrett, Orca Network online, accessed at http://www.orcanetwork.org/captivity/keikostory.html.

Appendix VII. D.

1. "Killer dolphins?" Steve Chapple, (c) Christian Science Monitor, printed in the *Anchorage Daily News* Dec. 9, 1977, page 1, accessed at http://news.google.com/newspapers?nid=1828&dat=19771209&id=gzEeAAAAIBAJ&sjid=Ub4EAAAAIBAJ&pg=1028,1171456 on 10/16/12.

2. "The US Navy's Deadly MK6 Attack Dolphin Program," Brandon Webb, June 25, 2012, accessed athttp://sofrep.com/8496/the-us-navys-mk-6-attack-dolphins/?utm_source=rssht on 10/16/12; "Navy Dolphins," Frontline, transcript, interview with Ric O'Barry, accessed at http://www.pbs.org/wgbh/pages/frontline/shows/whales/etc/robarry.html on 10/16/12; "In the Matter of: Richard O'Barry," U.S. Department of Commerce, National Oceanic and Atmospheric Administration, Office of the Administrative Law Judge, case details, 1999, accessed at http://www.animallaw.info/cases/caus1999noaalexis1.htm on 10/16/12.

3. See "The US Navy's Deadly MK 6 Attack Dolphin Program," Webb, posted June 25, 2012, accessed at http://sofrep.com/8496/the-us-navys-mk-6-attack- dolphins/#ixzz28FkRWLIf on 10/8/12.

4. "A Brief History of the Navy's Marine Mammal Program," a chapter in SSC San Diego TD 627, Revision D, Annotated Bibliography of Publications from the U.S. Navy's Marine Mammal Program, May 1998, accessed at http://www.spawar.navy.mil/sti/publications/ pubs/td/627/index.html on 10/16/12; "Miscellaneous," a resource list at Annotated Bibliography of Publications from the U.S. Navy's Marine Mammal Program, May 1998, accessed at http://www.spawar.navy.mil/sti/publications/pubs/td/627/revd/ch11misc. html on 10/16/12.

ACKNOWLEDGMENTS

T HE AUTHOR ACKNOWLEDGES THAT HIS LIFE AND THE special circumstance that allowed him to arrive at this point and complete this book project was due to many wonderful people. This book was possible only because of the help and selfless support of close friends, family members, professors, mentors, Navy civil servants, officers and men. As with many significant life events, this project required lots of luck and the Grace of God.

To list all the individuals who contributed to this book would take pages.

However, I will first acknowledge those who shaped my life and mentored me: Harold and Margaret Goforth, Sharon Goforth and our lovely family, Dr. Curry T. Haynes, Dr. E. Lowe Pierce, Dr. Frank Friedl, Dr. V. Reggie Edgerton, Bill B. Quigley, and Bill A. Powell. Secondly, those who tolerated my frequent questioning that challenged their fading memories to recall important details: Bill Powell, Dan Hightower, Bill Scronce, Larry Phillips, Sam Ridgway, Les Bivens, Chris Frier, Dave Ussery, Hop Porter, Clark Bowers, Bob Bailey, Don McSheehy, Milo McManus, Bill Steele, Blair Irvine, Mike Schultz, Jim Corey, Doug Murphy, Terry Rioux, Walter Moore, Chuck Chaldekas, Liz Babcock, and Tom LaPuzza. Thirdly, those who provided photos, approvals, and documents: Edward Budzyna, Edward Roper, Terry Rioux, Bob Bailey, Bill Scronce, Sam Ridgway, Ray Smith, Jim Corey, Mark Xitco, Brett Burner and Dolores Powell.

I especially acknowledge Anita K. Palmer, the saint who was my expert editor and kept this project moving forward. She never gave up and kept saying, Hal this is going to be a good story.

ABOUT THE AUTHOR

I N 1969, HAROLD (HAL) GOFORTH, JR. WAS THE FIRST military person to join the secret project that would become Project Short Time. For two years he lived and breathed dolphin training, deploying to Vietnam to serve at Cam Ranh Bay until his tour ended in June 1971.

Goforth grew up in Florida with a love for water, swimming, fishing, and science. After earning a Bachelor of Science degree in Biology from the University of Florida (1966), he joined the Navy in February 1967 as the Vietnam War was escalating. He graduated from Officer Candidate School, and became a diver and Explosive Ordinance Disposal officer, making the rank of lieutenant on active duty. His long-term goal always was to become a marine biologist.

After leaving active duty, Goforth earned a Master's degree in Zoology at the University of South Florida, Tampa (1973) and a Ph.D. in Kinesiology at the University of California Los Angeles (1986).

From 1973 to 1986, he worked as a marine scientist at the Naval Ocean Systems Center, San Diego, Marine Sciences Division. He was a research physiologist and department head at the Naval Health Research Center, San Diego from 1986 to 2000. As an adjunct associate professor, he taught marine sciences and exercise physiology at Point Loma Nazarene University from 1992 to 2010.

Goforth has been published in numerous research journals, reports, conference proceedings and books. He is a member of; the American College of Sports Medicine (ACSM, Fellow Emeritus), Society for Marine Mammalogy, International Marine Animal Trainers Association and Navy and Marine Corps Explosive Ordnance Disposal Association and UDT-SEAL Association.

His reserve duty lasted twenty-two years from 1971 to 1993. He retired from the Navy after 26+ years with the rank of Navy Captain.

A long-distance runner, Goforth competed in fifty marathons, running in the Boston Marathon in thirty-four consecutive years (qualifying every year) and placing in the top three of his age division seven times. He and his wife, Sharon, have been married forty-eight years, and have three adult children and three grand-children. Because of this, they divide their time between San Diego and South Florida.

The author with Toad. San Diego, 2006. *(U.S. Navy. Used by permission.)*

CPSIA information can be obtained
at www.ICGtesting.com
Printed in the USA
FSHW04n1545070318
45215FS